'This inspiring book, *Stories fro[m]* [the Streets by Luke] Randall and Sue Shaw serves as [a reminder of the] difference we can make in the liv[es of others. It can] sometimes seem quite simple ac[tions ... we can see] the size of the need and feel inadequate in what we can do to help. What this book does is remind us all of how a series of ordinary acts can have a significant impact. I wonder how many lives have been helped, and on occasions even saved, by those mentioned in this book, who have faithfully invested their time and energy in looking out for others ... may it inspire you to do the same!'
Ryan Ahern, Pastor, Esher Green Baptist Church

'Luke and Sue take us on a gripping journey across the UK and to Antigua, as we hear the stories of the frontline volunteers motivated by the compassion of Jesus Christ – which is the heart and soul of Street Pastors. We see God's dignity – caring, helping and listening – in a world where it is in short supply, whether in a one-off conversation with a vulnerable late-night reveller or life-saving words to a suicidal homeless person. It refreshingly inspires us at a time when we have been locked out of church buildings to get out there and be the living body of Christ (as one volunteer said, "God's hands, His eyes and His feet") in our streets, railway stations and schools.'
David Burrowes, Former MP for Enfield Southgate (2005-2017)
and Patron of Ascension Trust

'*Stories from the Streets* allows us a snapshot from around the UK and Antigua of all the amazing work that Street Pastors are doing. As you read the book you can sense the passion of the volunteers, the genuine caring, listening and helping that they all do and their desire to be the light in the

darkness, knowing that God goes before them in all situations. It is also great to read the acknowledgements from the general public, the police, and so on, with regard to the great work the Street Pastors do.'
Sally Leonard, Reading Street Pastors Coordinator 2012 to present

'*Stories from the Streets* does "what it says on the tin". It provides blow-by-blow accounts of what it is really like to "love your neighbour" by caring, listening, helping – the Street Pastors' motto.

'Whether you are already a Street Pastor, in training or considering how to be a better Good Samaritan, you will find *Stories from the Streets* a helpful resource.'
Teresa James, Street Pastors leader since 2006

'An impressive narrative on the life of Street Pastors. The authors have clearly spent time doing background research and have significant experience of patrolling the streets themselves.'
Barry Sebastian, Street Pastors Coordinator, Antigua

STORIES FROM THE STREETS

An insight into the work of Street Pastors

Dr Luke Randall and Sue Shaw

instant apostle

First published in Great Britain in 2020

Instant Apostle
The Barn
1 Watford House Lane
Watford
Herts
WD17 1BJ

British Library Cataloguing-in-Publication Data

A catalogue record for this book is available from the British Library.

This book and all other Instant Apostle books are available from Instant Apostle:

Website: www.instantapostle.com

Email: info@instantapostle.com

ISBN 978-1-912726-28-8

Printed in Great Britain.

Dedication

Dr Luke Randall would like to dedicate this book to his brother and sister, Seb and Rose, and their families, to the Street Pastors family and to rough sleepers, some of whom Street Pastors meet on the streets.

Sue Shaw would like to dedicate this book to the Street Pastors family, especially Street Pastors Antigua, and to the rough sleepers of St John's, Antigua.

Contents

Foreword

The Church is a force for good in the world and it is represented by a body of people who exhibit a rich history of caring for the poor, the weak and the vulnerable in our society. The Street Pastors initiative reflects this relevance of the Church and, even more importantly, of Christ and His gospel.

Stories from the Streets seeks to demonstrate and celebrate this relevance by highlighting the excellence and the transformative power of the work being done by what I can only describe as a formidable army of Street Pastors who have become a welcome presence in their various battalions in towns and cities across our nation. The book captures the excitement and the passion of all the volunteers who serve as Street Pastors as well as the gratitude of those with whom they come into contact. The stories also remind us that God is in the business of taking ordinary people and using them in powerful and practical ways.

I started Street Pastors in Brixton in 2003. I was inspired by a model that I saw in Jamaica, where individual churches joined together to take their presence and values out onto the streets. We started in London by providing practical help to people engaging with the night-time economy. Our work included handing out space blankets[1] outside nightclubs, as well as flip flops to clubbers who were unable to walk home in their high heels. We also gave out drinking water, chocolate for those low on energy, personal alarms and bus timetables, and assisted others to call taxis to get home. In some cases, as a last resort, we were able to facilitate access to sleeping bags stored in churches. Our teams would also remove bottles and other potential weapons from the streets in order to discourage violence and vandalism, and they were there to generally ensure the safety of those who were out on the streets and vulnerable.

Over the past seventeen years, Street Pastors has expanded its reach nationally and internationally and has developed partner initiatives, including School Pastors (who mentor young people in schools and work to reduce bullying, antisocial behaviour and drug use, as well as to help to remove barriers to learning), Rail Pastors (who work to prevent suicide attempts and fatalities on the railway) and Response Pastors (who support those who are affected by disaster or crisis). To date, there are 270 active Street Pastors groups nationally and seven internationally,[2] and together they have worked with more than 12,000 volunteers, with a phenomenal level of commitment and hard work that testifies to the robustness and relevance of so many

---

[1] Foil blankets.

[2] https://www.streetpastors.org/our-network/united-kingdom/ (accessed 10th September 2020)

churches that I have had the pleasure of working with over the years and the hundreds of amazing individuals who make up those congregations.

There are so many stories that have not been captured in this small volume, but it is my hope that those that have been included will remind us of the impact that the Church is having on the streets of the United Kingdom every weekend. Furthermore, it is my hope that these stories may inspire our current Street Pastors not to become 'weary in doing good' because 'at the proper time', they 'will reap a harvest' (Galatians 6:9, NIV UK). And I also hope that they may inspire a new generation of volunteers to take up the mantle of becoming Street Pastors, since volunteerism is the lifeblood of what we do.

For myself, if I ever find myself in any doubt about the Church's impact through the Street Pastors initiatives, I should only have to pick up this volume and browse through it to remind myself of why we have been doing what we do for so many years, and why we will continue to do it. One of the most recent stories that highlights the value of the work for me is the recognition that was given to the Preston Street Pastors group, in July 2020, for their service to the community and the group being voted as the number one charity to go on the city's new monopoly board. That is impactful! And a real tribute to the men and women who serve in Preston.

I would like to express my gratitude to Sue and Luke for gathering these wonderful stories and for sharing them with us and with all those who read this book. May they encourage us all to know that we have a role to play in making our society and nation a great place to live!

Les Isaac, summer 2020

Preface

Rev Les Isaac's (CEO and founder of Street Pastors) first book on Street Pastors was published in 2009 and is simply called *Street Pastors*.[3] His second book, published in 2014, was called *Faith on the Streets*.[4] With two books already published about Street Pastors, why another book?

One night, in my first year of being a Street Pastor, a man came up to the team in the early hours of the morning and asked, 'But what do you actually do?' He gave the impression that he had only ever seen Street Pastors just walking around. The man seemed a bit the worse for drink, but did not need help from us.

The team leader for the night replied something like, 'We're here to make sure you all get home safely.'

This book is in one sense a more complete answer to that man's question. While Rev Les Isaac has answered that man's question in his two books, this book gives a different perspective, having been written by volunteer Street Pastors. It also updates *Faith on the Streets* by

---

[3] Les Isaac and Rosalind Davies, *Street Pastors* (Colorado Springs, CO: David C Cook, 2009).

[4] Les Isaac and Rosalind Davies, *Faith on the Streets: Christians in Action Through the Street Pastors Movement* (London: Hodder & Stoughton, 2014).

incorporating some material on Response and Rail Pastors and School Pastors, focuses on new encounters and stories not told in previous books, outlines the work of group coordinators in five different locations and includes stories about Street Pastors in Antigua.

Although many evenings may involve no more than friendly conversations, other evenings may involve interactions that lead to life-changing or life-saving stories. There are stories about different Street Pastors, the homeless, rough sleepers, other members of the public, and more.

Whatever your reasons for reading this book, hopefully you will find parts of interest to you.

To respect confidentiality, no real names of members of the public or their pets are used, unless permission has been given to use a first name only. Additionally, for several areas depicted, the names of towns or cities are not given and, in most cases, street and venue names are not stated.

If deemed necessary, to protect confidentiality, the peripheral details of a few stories have been changed. In some cases, the names of individual Street Pastors are given with their permission.

Informal conversations with members of the public are accurate with respect to general meaning. However, such conversations have been recalled from memory and are not word for word as they were spoken. Additionally, written stories sent in may have had minor edits with the authors' consent.

Acknowledgements

The authors would like to thank Street, Rail, Response and School Pastors from the UK and beyond who make the work of Street Pastors possible, and freely give their time to care, listen and help.

We would also like to thank:

- All of those who gave stories and/or information that have been used in this book, including two stories from former homeless people.

- Street Pastors team coordinators Andy Amour (Edinburgh), Roy Beaumont (Plymouth), Stuart Crawford (Glasgow), Sally Leonard (Reading) and Adrian Prior-Sankey (Taunton) for extensive material.

- Sarah Williams, a Street Pastors trainer who wrote the chapter 'Safety on the Streets'.

- Chris Lincoln, who wrote the chapter on Street Pastors in the north-east of England, and provided material on Response Pastors.

- Wilhelmina Barton, for stories from Northern Ireland.

- Clare Constant, Jeanette Holt and Georgina Randall for reading the manuscript and making editorial comments.

- Members of the public, who often show Street Pastors huge support and thanks, which is a real encouragement.

- Those who work in the night-time economy, in particular ambulance crews, door staff and the police, who can often be hugely supportive of Street Pastors teams and the situations they encounter.

- Organisations that work to support and help the homeless, to which Street Pastors can signpost individuals as needed.

- Organisations and agencies that support Street Pastors with funding.

- The publishers, Instant Apostle, for giving us confidence to pursue writing the book and in getting it published.

Finally, we would like to thank Ascension Trust, the umbrella body for Street Pastors, and Rev Les Isaac (CEO and founder of Street Pastors) for giving us permission to share these stories.

Introduction

Street Pastors was founded in 2003 by Rev Les Isaac, but it sits under the umbrella organisation Ascension Trust, also started by Les Isaac some years earlier in 1993.

Ascension Trust aims to empower churches to be effective as 'salt and light'[5] in their local communities. Taken from its website in 2019, this is how Ascension Trust describes its core values.[6]

Ascension Trust is a Christian inter-denominational organisation with a passion to mobilise the Church to make a positive contribution to society and to improve the quality of life of the disadvantaged and vulnerable.

Combining the skills and professional expertise of likeminded Christians and non-Christians, we aim to develop and implement practical and effective strategies to transform lives.

To continue mobilising and training volunteers to serve communities and work with the marginalised in

---

[5] Matthew 5:13-14.

[6] Ascension Trust, 'Mission and Core Values', https://www.ascensiontrust.org.uk/about-us/mission-core-values/ (accessed 8th July 2020).

society to increase our impact in communities and help create savings for the public purse.

But how does Street Pastors fit into the Christian heritage of the past in the UK, and how does it fit into society today alongside similar organisations?

In his 2015 book *The Mansion House of Liberty: The Untold Story of Christian Britain*, the author, John Bradley, addresses the immensely important contribution Christianity has made to the development of British society, institutions and values.[7] The author starts in AD100-200 and traces the influence of Christianity in law, parliament, the economy, the relief of poverty, healthcare and prison reform, women's rights and statues, liberty and free speech and more.

Moving to the present, the author refers to a speech made in 2009 by Archbishop of York, John Sentamu, in which he urged, 'Let's draw upon the riches of our heritage and find a sense of purpose for those who are thrashing around for meaning and settling for second best.'[8] John Sentamu has in the past praised the work of Street Pastors by saying, 'Street Pastors works because it recognises our common humanity and common responsibility in bringing hope to the communities we share.'[9]

---

[7] John Bradley, *The Mansion House of Liberty: The Untold Story of Christian Britain* (Weybridge: RoperPenberthy Publishing, 2015).

[8] Archbishop John Sentamu, 'The Triumphs of Englishness', lecture delivered at the Sunday Times Literary Festival in Oxford, 2009.

[9] Spring Harvest News Easter 2013, https://issuu.com/springharvest/docs/shnewsspring13 (accessed 8th July 2020).

In the final chapter of the book, the author comments, 'The Christian faith is of little avail if its values, morality and practice are not reflected in the lives of its adherents. Conversely, it can be a force for good when Christians live out their faith practically.'[10]

One force for good in the last 150 years that grew out of the Christian heritage of Britain and has had an influence across the world is The Salvation Army. The Salvation Army was founded in 1865 in London by one-time Methodist circuit-preacher William Booth and his wife, Catherine, as the East London Christian Mission, tracing its origins to the Blind Beggar tavern.[11]

The Salvation Army now reports a worldwide membership of more than 1.7 million,[12] operating in 130 countries.[13] It is widely known for running charity shops, operating shelters for the homeless and disaster relief and humanitarian aid to developing countries.

Although The Salvation Army began more than 150 years ago, it remains relevant in today's culture. One recent example of this relevance is that since 2011, The Salvation Army has been the government's official provider of anti-trafficking services in England and

---

[10] Bradley, *The Mansion House of Liberty*, p 245.

[11] The Salvation Army, 'Transforming Lives since 1865 – The story of The Salvation Army so far', https://story.salvationarmy.org (accessed 8th July 2020).

[12] The Salvation Army International, 'Statistics, the Countries Where the Salvation Army is at work',
https://web.archive.org/web/20180314174058/https:/www.salvationarmy.org/ihq/statistics (accessed 8th July 2020).

[13] The Salvation Army, 'The Salvation Army's Work Extends to 130 Countries', https://salvationarmy.ca/blog/the-salvation-armys-work-extends-to-130-countries/ (accessed 8th July 2020).

Wales, and has helped more than 7,000 victims of modern slavery.[14]

Another example of the relevance of The Salvation Army to society today was its involvement in the United States following the tragedy of 9/11, when it was present to provide comfort and support to victims, families of victims and relief workers, and was involved in feeding and hydration services around the clock.[15] John Berglund was responsible for emergency services in The Salvation Army's Southwest Division when he was deployed to Ground Zero.[16] In an interview in 2014 he said, 'The Salvation Army will always be noted historically for the service it provided in New York, but more importantly, The Salvation Army will be remembered by the individual lives it touched.'[17]

Street Pastors has more recent beginnings than The Salvation Army, and has only been established at present for less than twenty years. In this short time, Street Pastors has rapidly gained respect across the UK and in a number of other countries, showing itself to be relevant to today's culture. Street Pastors are a recognised and trusted part of the night-time economy in hundreds of towns and cities in the UK, and are also respected in their roles as Rail, Response and School Pastors, which are

---

covered to some extent in this book. Perhaps some day Street Pastors will grow as big as The Salvation Army movement?

The role of Street Pastors is complementary to and not in competition with organisations such as The Salvation Army. While The Salvation Army is at its heart a Protestant Church, as well as an international charitable organisation,[18] Street Pastors is not a church, but rather draws its volunteers from the entire spectrum of Protestant and Catholic churches that are or could be members of Churches Together in England.[19] This has a uniting effect across different church types. Volunteers from different church backgrounds, such as Catholic, Pentecostal, Anglican, Baptist and many more, may find themselves working together to 'care, listen and help', or perhaps, as Jesus put it, 'Love others as well as you love yourself.'[20]

Indeed, Street Pastors provides training and a structure whereby Christians can get out of the four walls of their church to help their neighbours, and volunteers can be from eighteen years old to eighty-plus years old; there is no upper age limit for volunteers.

A woman in her early seventies from the south of England summarises briefly her experiences of being a Street Pastor:

---

[18] The Salvation Army, 'Transforming lives since 1865 – The story of The Salvation Army so far', https://story.salvationarmy.org (accessed 8th July 2020).

[19] Churches Together in England, https://www.cte.org.uk (accessed 16th July 2020).

[20] Mark 12:31.

Hi, I'm Wendy, I've been a Street Pastor for two and a half years and I can honestly say it's been a life-changing experience for me.

I used to avoid going into the town where I patrol as a Street Pastor on a Friday or Saturday night, but now I look forward to it; to seeing young people out enjoying themselves, to chat with them, but to help them too. We give out lollypops to any who want them and flip flops to women who are hobbling out of the nightclubs in their high heels. If people have had too much to drink, we make sure they are alright, give them bottles of water and stay with them until they are sober enough to get a cab home.

They are always so grateful and remember it was Street Pastors who helped them. We are often greeted with hugs and sometimes with expressions such as, 'We love you!' and, 'You saved my life!'

Seeing so many rough sleepers is sad, but it's good to be able to help them with sleeping bags, clothes, sandwiches and even books to read. We also offer support to newly homeless people. We tell them about the local night shelters where they can get a hot meal, and a local charity that helps them get accommodation.

No two nights are the same; it really is a most interesting and rewarding experience to volunteer as a Street Pastor.

It is unfortunate to be saying this, but good too, because by going out regularly at weekends, we build up a relationship with the homeless. We greet them by name and ask after their health, their situation and whether it has changed, and ask what we can do to help. I have found this has also changed my attitude to all homeless people that I encounter during the day – I now smile and say, 'Hello,' whereas before I might have walked by without a sideways glance. I now buy *The Big Issue* and stop to have a chat. I have built up a relationship with one *Big Issue* woman, where we pray for each other each week when I stop to buy my copy. I would never have done this before I became a Street Pastor – it has changed me.

Chapter 1
The Story of the Good Samaritan

Thankfully, it was a dry autumn evening. Our patrol hadn't been that eventful when we came across a man, perhaps in his early sixties, whose hands were bleeding profusely. To our surprise and disappointment, he refused all our offers of first aid. We finally managed to persuade him to take some of our antiseptic wipes and plasters, in case he decided to clean himself up (we later found out that he had in fact self-harmed). As we were reluctantly about to go, he asked us, 'Why do you guys do what you do?'

We simply told him, 'Because you're worth it.'

It was as if a light had been switched on; a smile appeared on his face and a tear in his eye. He made a point of thanking each of us individually and we went away grateful to have perhaps played a part in him realising something of his true worth.

This short story represents in a nutshell why Street Pastors do what they do, because everyone has true worth. This worth is not related to our bank balance, education, correct lifestyle choices and behaviours, heritage or looks. Christians believe the true worth of each one of us lies in the fact that we are made 'in the image of God'[21] and bear the stamp of our creator.

Another Street Pastor recounts this story:

One night we noticed a group of about six women standing around something on the ground, and behaving in a greatly agitated manner. They were standing around another woman, their friend, who was lying in the recovery position on the pavement. One woman was kneeling next to her trying to do something to help her.

'She's not breathing; I can't hear her breathing,' she called out in desperation.

'She's going to die,' another said.

'Is she dead? Is she dead?' asked another.

Yet another called out, 'Somebody do something.'

It seemed like that somebody was going to be me. I quickly shut out thoughts of the awful possible outcomes and resisted the panic rising inside me. All that training... 'Time to move up a gear,' I told myself.

'What's her name?' I asked.

'Becky,' replied one of the women.

'Becky, my name is Joe, I'm a Street Pastor, I want to help you. Can you hear me?' No reply. I tried again; still no reply or any form of response. I tried to hear her breathing, but it was too noisy.

There was a Street Pastor standing next to me. I looked up. 'Peter, please try to quieten them. I can't hear a thing. I'm trying to hear if she's breathing.

---

[21] See Genesis 1:27 (NIV UK).

There's still too much noise, the women and the traffic.'

I turned Becky on her back and tried to detect chest movement indicating breathing... nothing. But she was not dead. 'She has a weak but steady pulse,' I shouted to anybody who needed to know.

A member of our team called Julie had replaced Peter and was kneeling next to me. 'Julie, is your phone handy?' She nodded. 'Call 999 and ask for an ambulance; tell them she's not breathing, answer their questions and relay to them what you see.'

For a moment that seemed like minutes, I thought, 'What do I do now? Is she shamming? Is she sleepy, soporific from the alcohol? Is she just taking time out? Do I give her CPR?'[22]

And then came the realisation – if I did nothing, she might die. I recalled all those weeks of training. Check the mouth for obstructions – nothing there. Check her neck and wrist for a Medi-Alert medallion – nothing.

'Does anyone know her?' I asked as loudly as I could. One of the young women came forward. 'What's your name?'

'Sam,' she replied.

'Sam, does your friend have any medical conditions you know about?'

'No.'

'Does she have a pacemaker?'

'Not that I know about.'

I decided to start doing CPR. Becky coughed twice, so I stopped compressions, checked her mouth for

---

[22] Cardiopulmonary resuscitation.

any obstruction that might have come loose –
nothing. She still wasn't breathing.

I resumed compressions; 'One-two-three-four-
five…'

Becky coughed again, and then groaned aloud,
'Stop it, that hurts.' Becky was not only breathing; she
was also talking.

'*Phew*, I did it. We did it.'

At that moment a paramedic car pulled up and
two paramedics got out. I briefed them on what had
happened and they gladly took over looking after
Becky. After a few minutes, and when Becky seemed
to be stable and in the capable care of the paramedics,
I asked if we could go. With their permission, the
team left the scene and went off into the night, to
meet the next unknown of our weekend vigil.

In the preface to the book *Faith on the Streets*, David
Burrowes (Conservative Member of Parliament for
Enfield Southgate from 2005 to 2017 and Patron of
Ascension Trust, the umbrella body for Street Pastors)
refers to the story of the Good Samaritan. Both of the
above stories share some parts in common with that
story. Someone in need was helped by a stranger, who
chose not to ignore them. The story of the Good
Samaritan is one of the most well-known stories that
Jesus told:

'There was once a man traveling from Jerusalem to
Jericho. On the way he was attacked by robbers. They
took his clothes, beat him up, and went off leaving
him half-dead. Luckily, a priest was on his way down
the same road, but when he saw him he angled across

to the other side. Then a Levite religious man showed up; he also avoided the injured man.

'A Samaritan traveling the road came on him. When he saw the man's condition, his heart went out to him. He gave him first aid, disinfecting and bandaging his wounds. Then he lifted him onto his donkey, led him to an inn, and made him comfortable. In the morning he took out two silver coins and gave them to the innkeeper, saying, "Take good care of him. If it costs any more, put it on my bill – I'll pay you on my way back."

'What do you think? Which of the three became a neighbor to the man attacked by robbers?'

'The one who treated him kindly,' the religion scholar responded.

Jesus said, 'Go and do the same.'[23]

In the story, it is the despised Samaritan and not the priest or the Levite (religious person of the day) who chooses to help the man in need. In doing so, the Samaritan acts like a neighbour or friend to the injured man.

The story of the Good Samaritan is allegorical. However, similar true stories no doubt happen all around the world on a regular basis, such as the two at the start of this chapter. Like the title of this book, the story of the Good Samaritan is a story from the streets.

Since Jesus told this story, there have been countless expositions and sermons about it, and it has been

---

[23] Luke 10:30-37.

interpreted in different ways. Martin Luther King Jnr said of this parable:

> On the one hand we are called to play the Good Samaritan on life's roadside, but that will be only an initial act. One day we must come to see that the whole Jericho road must be transformed so that men and women will not be constantly beaten and robbed as they make their journey on life's highway. True compassion is more than flinging a coin to a beggar; it is not haphazard and superficial. It comes to see that an edifice which produces beggars needs restructuring.[24]

Now, about 2,000 years after Jesus told this story, the word 'Samaritan' has become part of the name of charities, hospitals and clinics around the world. Probably the best known of these in the UK is the organisation Samaritans itself.

Samaritans was founded in 1953 by a vicar who offered counselling to his parishioners, but wanted to do more to help people struggling to cope and possibly contemplating suicide. By the simple act of listening and offering non-judgemental support, Samaritans is able to offer a safe space, so people can talk and be listened to without judgement. The success of this initiative has led to Samaritans now having more than 200 branches across

[24] Douglas A Hicks and Mark R Valeri, *Global Neighbors: Christian Faith and Moral Obligation in Today's Economy* (Grand Rapids, MI: Eerdmans Publishing Company, 2008), p 31.

the UK and Republic of Ireland.[25] Samaritans' 20,000 volunteers are available at any time for anyone who is struggling to cope. Samaritans currently responds to more than five million requests for help a year,[26] and no doubt has been involved in saving thousands of lives since the charity started.

Another example of the use of the word 'Samaritan' by a charity that seeks to help is Samaritan's Purse. Samaritan's Purse is an international relief and development organisation that started in 1970.[27] Samaritan's Purse operates in Africa, Eastern Europe and Central Asia, with offices in the UK, the USA, Canada, Germany and Australia. Samaritan's Purse is probably best known for Operation Christmas Child. Between 1990 and 2020, shoeboxes full of gifts have been given to more than 178 million children in more than 160 countries via this initiative.[28]

The Good Samaritan story has no doubt been inspirational in the lives of many. For many it provides the inspiration to make the journey from being a person wanting to help others, but not wanting to be potentially corrupted or contaminated by someone in need of help (as the religious people in the story saw it), to someone

[25] Samaritans, https://www.samaritans.org/about-samaritans/our-organisation/our-governance-and-structure/ (accessed 10th September 2020).

[26] GOV.UK, 'PM pledges action on suicide to mark World Mental Health Day', https://www.gov.uk/government/news/pm-pledges-action-on-suicide-to-mark-world-mental-health-day (accessed 8th July 2020).

[27] Samaritans Purse, https://www.samaritans-purse.org.uk (accessed 8th July 2020).

[28] Ibid.

who gets involved to care and help, realising that, in one sense, all people are our neighbours.

Mother Teresa, an example to many, is perhaps one of the best-known examples of an individual who has been described as a modern-day Good Samaritan. She was someone who genuinely cared for the destitute, irrespective of their background.

A favourite motto of Mother Teresa was, 'Do small things with great love.'[29] The 'small things' she did so captivated the world that she was given honorary degrees and other awards, was praised by the media and was sought out by dignitaries.[30] Although she had calls on her time from all over the world, she always returned to India, to be with those she loved most – the lonely, abandoned, homeless, disease-ravaged, dying, 'poorest of the poor'.[31]

Street Pastors was pioneered in London in 2003 by Rev Les Isaac and had small beginnings. On the first night out in April 2003, eighteen volunteers, comprising fifteen women and three men, took to the streets of Brixton. This first night out was just a few months after four teenage girls were shot, two fatally, in Birmingham. Concerns about gun and knife crime were part of the impetus for starting Street Pastors (read *Faith on the Streets* for more details).

---

[29] Catholic News Service. 'Mother Teresa: Do small things with great love', https://www.cny.org/stories/st-teresado-small-things-with-great-love,14390? (accessed 10th September 2020).
[30] Ibid.
[31] Ibid.

Since this first night, by 2020 more than 12,000 Street and Prayer Pastors have been trained in the UK, who have played an active part in strengthening community life and working for safer streets.[32] Currently (2020), there are 270 active Street Pastors groups in towns and cities around the UK. Additionally, in 2020 Street Pastors are operating in Australia, the Channel Islands (Jersey), Gibraltar, Ireland, Nigeria, the USA and the West Indies (Antigua, Jamaica, Trinidad and Tobago).[33]

The main role of Street Pastors is summarised as 'caring, listening and helping'. While Les Isaac may not have been specifically inspired by the story of the Good Samaritan to start Street Pastors, he was responding to need in the same way as the Samaritan did, doing something to help others in need rather than ignoring the issues.

When Christians focus their efforts on issues of social justice, such as economic inequality, poverty, alcoholism, crime, racial tensions, slums, child labour, inadequate labour unions, poor schools and the like, this can be termed 'the social gospel'.[34] The social gospel as a phrase was first used in the late nineteenth century in America and was then a movement in North American Protestantism, applying Christian ethics to social problems.[35] The social gospel is said to have peaked in

---

[32] Street Pastors, https://www.streetpastors.org (accessed 8th July 2020).
[33] Ibid.
[34] Learn Religions, 'A Deep Dive Into the History of the Social Gospel Movement', https://www.learnreligions.com/social-gospel-movement-4136473 (accessed 16th July 2020).
[35] Martin Marty, *Modern American Religion. Volume 1: The Irony of It All, 1893–1919* (Chicago, IL: University of Chicago Press, 1997).

the early part of the twentieth century, but the principles continue to inspire newer movements,[36] such as Christians Against Poverty.[37]

While people see Jesus' life and concern for the poor, and His teaching, for example in the story of the Good Samaritan, as a clear mandate for social gospel-type action, the social gospel has its critics. In Rev Les Isaac's book *Faith on the Streets*, the question is asked, 'Why do Christians sometimes debate whether "words" or "actions" are more important to the presentation of the message of Jesus?' One of the concerns raised was, 'Doesn't putting emphasis on social action take the edge off preaching the gospel?'[38]

In a *Church Times* article on the social gospel in 2016, the author commented:

The movement's mission became detached from its theological core, becoming, in effect, indistinguishable from any other social action. For wholly admirable, if ultimately misguided, reasons, love of neighbour eclipsed love of God. This remains a danger today. If one is not careful, God becomes little more than Good, or, even worse, feel-good.[39]

---

[36] Christopher H Evans, *The Social Gospel Today* (Louisville, KY: Westminster John Knox Press, 2001).

[37] https://capuk.org/ (accessed 10th September 2020).

[38] Isaac and Davies, *Faith on the Streets*, p 85.

[39] Nick Spencer, 'From social action to social liturgy', *Church Times*, 22nd December 2016, https://www.churchtimes.co.uk/articles/2016/23-december/comment/opinion/from-social-action-to-social-liturgy (accessed 8th July 2020).

However, the article's title was 'From social action to social liturgy'. The article went on to comment:

> The word 'liturgy' is commonly understood to mean 'church worship', but the New Testament Greek word from which it derives, *leitourgia*, could be used to mean both priestly service within the Temple, and public charitable activity.[40]

> 'Social liturgy', then, is not simply social action that is devoid of any serious theological formation, nor Christian 'worship' that loves God and ignores one's neighbour. It is, rather, the practice of public commitment to the other that is explicitly rooted in, and shaped by, love of God; working for and 'being with' the other while being deliberately God-conscious or priestly.[41]

Interestingly, the article commended the work of Street Pastors by saying, 'Their presence diffuses tension and aggression in a way that the police find difficult to do.'[42]

Jackie Pullinger, who set up a work in 1966 helping drug addicts and the poor in Hong Kong,[43] gave an interview that was published in *Premier Christianity* magazine.[44] In this interview, she commented that she had 'thought that preaching the gospel was explaining

---

[40] Ibid.

[41] Ibid.

[42] Ibid.

[43] Jackie Pullinger, *Chasing the Dragon* (London: Hodder & Stoughton, 2006).

[44] Sam Hailes, 'Jackie Pullinger – Interview', *Premier Christianity* magazine, January 2019.

how Jesus came to die for your sins and, of course, that's not preaching the gospel at all'. She went on to explain the reason why she considered this was not the gospel at all: 'I found out people there were not listening anyway, they were watching to see how I acted, whether I really did love them. And if I really did love them, maybe God did really love them.'[45]

45 Ibid.

Chapter 2
Caring, Listening and Helping

Caring, listening and helping instantly sums up the work of Street Pastors. Out on the street during the night there are numerous opportunities to care for, listen to and help people who are vulnerable, who have mental health issues, who are lonely, who are at the end of their tether or who are feeling frightened or alone.

In the Gospels there are many instances where Jesus the Good Shepherd reached out to care for and help those on the edge of society, the outcasts like the leprosy sufferer and the blind beggar, the street prostitute, a woman perceived to be unclean, the poor and powerless.

Following Jesus' example, Street Pastors offer care to whoever is in need, regardless of their status or position in society. The following stories, all from the south-west of England, demonstrate how effective Street Pastors can be when they are willing to care, listen and help.

Caring

For a variety of reasons, some people perceive themselves as being worthless, unacceptable and unlovable. It may be because of unemployment, homelessness, addictions, abuse or rejection. Here Street

Pastors from south-west England recall helping those struggling to believe they are worth caring for.

A war veteran regrets

We were in for our break at base when there was a call over the radio to help a man outside one of the nightclubs, so we went to see if we could assist.

We found a young man cross-legged and bent over. He was asleep and it took us a while to get him to respond. We tried encouraging him to drink sips of water but he responded by pushing the bottle away.

'Leave me alone, I'm not worth it,' he said.

'You are worth it and I'm not going anywhere. You are quite vulnerable sitting here,' I replied. He put his head in his hands and sobbed.

Eventually he gave us his name and told us he wanted to die, as he did not 'want to see any more dead bodies'. Then he went quiet and we encouraged him to drink more water. We asked about home, but he kept saying he couldn't go home, that he didn't want to do this any more.

He started to disclose more and told us that he had come back from serving in Iraq three years earlier. He hated himself for what he had done there. I told him that his actions were not the actions of a bad person as he had stepped in to save others (which reminded me of Jesus).

I asked about his family.

'They don't understand.'

'Have you talked to them to help them understand?'

'No, I can't put that on to them.'

We managed to get him on his feet and then he said that he wanted to get home. We gave him a Street Pastors card and said to him if he ever needed to talk, there would be someone who would listen to him. We managed to get him a taxi and he gave us a hug.

'Thank you for everything you have done,' he said.

Later the office received a phone call from a truly grateful man who had woken up to find a Street Pastors card in his pocket and having vague memories of a team helping him. He said he was so grateful for the help he'd received and was in a much better frame of mind now.

He mentioned that he was suffering from post-traumatic stress disorder (PTSD) and that the counselling he'd received to date hadn't been much help. We told him about Resolution, a charity that specialises in PTSD for military personnel. He was really interested to hear that and thanked us again.

A fearful abuse survivor
We were approached by a man who said that there was a woman sat outside a shop who was crying. As we were heading there, closed-circuit TV (CCTV) radioed to tell us about the very same woman. Sure enough, we found her outside a closed shop. We approached and asked if she was alright and she started sharing with us.

She had moved from London, having split up with her boyfriend. She was homeless and had a general fear of all men. Her own father had sold her for sex when she was just eleven years old for beer money. Social Services had put her in the care of her mother, who she said threw her out at the age of twelve. Her boyfriend in London wanted her to become a sex worker but when she said 'No' he put a gun to her head and hit her with it.

She had escaped to our town as she was so scared. She said that only last week as she was sitting in a park, a man tried to seduce her and when she said 'No' he gave her a 'back hand' and called her some choice words.

Sobbing, she said she couldn't understand why we were even talking to her and helping. She told us she prayed every night and had asked Jesus into her heart. We told her we were helping because she was worth it and that we were there because we cared about her safety. She told us that we were her answer to prayer.

It was obvious that she had nowhere to stay, so we asked the Prayer Pastors to contact the Salvation Army, who were willing to take her in. She agreed to go but wanted the other female Street Pastor and myself to stay with her, so we all accompanied her to that safe place.

We thought she might not stay as she was so frightened, but she was reassured to find they had another woman sleeping in the chapel. Her face lit up when she saw the wooden cross on the table and then discovered that she would be seen by a female staff member on the Monday to help her further. God is so good!

A former prisoner
During the evening I met a guy in his late fifties holding a walking stick. I was standing on his left and he held his walking stick in his right hand. As a stranger walked towards him, he made to raise his stick, thinking the man wanted to fight him. I gently lowered the stick in his

hand and assured him the passer-by was not there to hurt him.

We discovered that this man had spent his childhood being beaten up by his parents on a regular basis. I felt for him and everything that he had been through. I could tell he had been hurt so many times. Every time someone came close, he began to raise his stick and I gently lowered it again. I assured him that the passers-by did not want to hit him or hurt him. It gradually began to dawn on him that if he did not try to hit them, they left him alone. Through his childhood experiences he assumed that everyone was out to attack him.

I encouraged him to see his walking stick as an aid to walking, not as a weapon. He revealed he had only just come out of jail and had been in and out of prison his whole life. He explained that it was because of previous injuries he now needed a walking stick.

I could see his heart was hurting, and that he wanted to change and believe that people were not just out to attack him.

Towards the end of the conversation he was just using his stick to lean on, and his fear of others was lessening. I hope our time helped him to stop this cycle of violence and understand how much God loves him.

A sex worker
A woman sex worker asked us for gloves for herself and her friend as it was a very cold night.

While we were getting the gloves out of the bag, she told us that she was still feeling pain from having accidentally sliced the top of her thumb off a few months earlier, so we offered to pray for healing, which she accepted.

As we prayed, she started to cry and asked if we could also pray for her friend there, as she had recently lost her father. That was OK with her friend and she too began to cry as we prayed. I like to think that it was the love of God touching them both that caused the tears.

Listening

James, one of Jesus' apostles, wrote in his letter, 'Lead with your ears, follow up with your tongue.'[46] His words could have been the other way round – speak first, listen last – but they weren't.

Dr Paul Tournier, a renowned twentieth-century Swiss physician, pastoral counsellor and author, wrote, 'No one can develop freely in this world and find a full life without feeling understood by at least one person.'[47]

Often in the small hours of the morning people will disclose their innermost thoughts and feelings with Street Pastors, as the following stories demonstrate. It is our prayer that as we listen to them, these people will become more fulfilled and whole.

'Where are you, God?'
We came across an older gentleman, who told us that his mum had died and that he had stood at her grave three weeks earlier, asking God, 'Where are you?'

---

[46] James 1:19.
[47] Paul Tournier, *To Understand Each Other* (Louisville, KY, Westminster John Knox Press, 1987), p 29.

He said that he was disappointed that God didn't answer, then he looked up and said, 'But I think He has now because He sent you guys to talk to me.'

This really touched my heart and I believe God put us in the right place at the right time to meet him.

'I don't want to wake up tomorrow morning'

Our update training was on Suicide Prevention and I read the leaflet while waiting to go out on patrol. During the second shift, we noticed a lone young woman sitting on a window ledge. She was hunched over, trying to make herself vomit. After using our tissues and taking some sips of water, she told me, 'I don't want to wake up tomorrow morning.'

I thought, 'It sounds as if I need to put my training into practice.'

'If I wasn't here no one would miss me for more than a few days,' she continued.

Remembering what I had just read and learned, I focused on discovering a reason for her to go on living, finding out her name, circumstances and current plans. She told me she worked in healthcare, and this gave me a good opportunity to emphasise the importance of her vital role in society.

Suddenly she seemed to find energy and phoned her friends, from whom she had become separated. They rapidly responded and I helped to direct them to where we were. Shortly afterwards their car pulled up and the woman rushed across the road and climbed into the back seat. I just had time to speak to a pleasant-looking woman in the passenger seat.

'Your friend has just told me that she is feeling low. Please keep an eye out for her.'

'Yes, we will,' she replied, and I felt confident that she would.

Helping

Picking up glass bottles; offering basic first aid; giving out flip flops; providing rough sleepers with a hat, scarf, pair of gloves; offering to accompany people home or on to public transport: there are a myriad of ways Street Pastors give practical help on the streets.

Sometimes when Street Pastors stop to help, their intervention prevents situations deteriorating. This can lead to unexpected and positive consequences, as these stories show.

Helping a police officer
We spent some time with a woman who was sat hunched in a doorway. We were concerned that she was being bothered by a man. She was very drunk and very confused. We wrapped a blanket around her shoulders and called over a police officer.

The stranger now realised that the woman had friends (albeit new ones) and walked off, but not before the police officer had taken his details. He told the officer that he'd met her inside a club and was only interested in her welfare, etc. However, when the officer returned to the police station and checked him out, he discovered that the stranger was a known sex offender.

We stayed with the young woman until her parents came to collect her. That night Street Pastors probably stopped something really dreadful from happening.

Helping club staff, police and ambulance
It was 2am one Sunday morning and we were returning to base for a break. As we passed a club, we saw a man, with blood all over his face and T-shirt, sitting on a pavement, being attended to by club door staff and others. We stopped to offer help.

He and his friends claimed he had been the victim of an unprovoked violent attack by a group of other lads, which was later substantiated by CCTV. The man had suffered repeated kicks to his ribs, had lost a tooth and was bleeding from a deep cut on his head.

The club staff were appreciative of us taking over, stemming the bleeding and helping him to cope with his injuries. He was very anxious and was also suffering with stomach problems.

We stayed with him until the police and an ambulance came on to the scene. Once the club staff had seen the video footage, they realised at least one of the lads involved in the attack was still on the premises and informed the police.

I am convinced it was the prayer of the Prayer Pastors, and the Street Pastors bringing God's loving, caring presence and peace into the situation, that encouraged the victim and his friends not to seek revenge on the attackers. The situation could have easily escalated into something much worse.

Instead, they waited for the police to arrive to deal with it, and as a second attacker emerged from the club, he was rapidly identified by the victim's friends and immediately taken into police custody.

We were so grateful to God for once more putting us in the right place at the right time and giving us the tools, the skills and the words not only to help others, but also to stop an already nasty situation becoming much worse.

Helping door staff

It was the last shift of the evening and the Street Pastors were informed that there was a car driving around the car park of a large nightclub with men 'tooled up' with knuckledusters and studded belts. The door staff felt that the presence of the Street Pastors would calm the situation, and one jokingly said, 'Can you pray that this place is cleared by 4am?'

The Street Pastors phoned in to base to request prayer for the situation and that the place be empty by 4am. With perhaps a little self-interest, the Prayer Pastors said that they would pray that it would be clear by 3.50am, so that the Street Pastors could get back to base and we could get away on time.

After ten minutes of hard prayer (note that getting away on time always focuses the mind), the Prayer Pastors received a phone call from the Street Pastors saying that a whole fleet of taxis had arrived and ferried everyone away, and there was no sign of the men in the car. The time? 3.50am precisely.

Unity

Street Pastors, regardless of their Christian tradition or location, are united by these qualities of caring, listening and helping. These essential qualities cross denominational boundaries, bringing together people from the whole spectrum of Christianity, from evangelicals to liberals. So, when people ask, 'Why do you do this?' Street Pastors can confidently say that they're following the example of Jesus, not promoting one particular denomination. The fact that Street Pastors are not trying to recruit people to join a church often makes quite an impact on people who are curious about the reasons we are out on the streets at night.

Chapter 3
Diary of a Night Out: Two Ambulances

Background

Looking back over ten years of being a Street Pastor, there have been many touching encounters, quite a few sad moments, some funny situations and occasional scary times.

Helping very intoxicated and potentially vulnerable young people can be difficult, but also hugely rewarding. Many scenarios are quite emotive, such as in the early hours of one freezing winter's morning when the team came across a young woman, dressed for a club but not for a winter's night, sitting alone on the pavement in a dark part of town. While conscious, whether through cold or intoxication or a combination, she was non-responsive. It took a female member of the team quite a while to get any response from her and encourage her to move out of the cold.

Eventually the young woman disclosed, 'I split up with my boyfriend tonight.'

The female team member gently asked, 'Can I use your phone to phone a friend or your family?'

It was great when her friend arrived to take care of her and give her a lift home.

Moving encounters have included getting to know homeless people. One homeless man who was wheelchair-bound and rough sleeping on occasions asked us, 'Can I pray for you and the team tonight?'

As we accepted his offer, he would hold our hands and pray for us. Sadly, he died a few years ago.

It was poignant to pray for a homeless woman one winter night as she sat on her sleeping bag in the semi-darkness of a town, surrounded by her few possessions. She told me in no uncertain terms, 'I really don't like religion,' but she accepted prayer. Tears formed in her eyes as we prayed for her.

Especially in the early years, I found it scary to be near to where a fight erupted, but I have never seen the team exposed to physical threat.

Watching physical aggression can be distressing, but thankfully it is not directed towards Street Pastors. Door staff and the police, when on the scene, do a terrific job at dealing with aggression.

There are lots of quite funny situations. People who have had a few drinks often see themselves as comedians.

Above all, it is often really encouraging that in general we get such a good response from the public and those who work in the night-time economy, particularly some fantastic door staff.

But what is it like to be out for a whole night? In the town where I am a Street Pastor, which has several large clubs, no two evenings are the same.

Evenings do have a general structure, though, which may change if we are involved with incidents. It is the people we meet and the situations that happen that make every evening varied. The structure of the evenings and the experiences of Street Pastors will be unique in different locations, depending on the type of town, its location, amenities and more.

Setting out for the night

Come with me as I describe a busy evening in a town in the South-East of England. Parts of this evening were similar to many others; parts were also unique.

We arrive at base about 9.30pm to get ready and always go out as a team of at least four. Preparation to go out most evenings in general sounds something like:

'Any volunteers to make the sandwiches tonight, please?'

'That's fine, we'll do that.'

'We need to stock up with lollies, flip flops, water and space blankets.'

'Has anyone checked the first aid bag? Who's first aid trained?'

'Who wants to carry the first aid bag? What about the bottles counter?'[48]

'Have you got the sandwiches for the homeless?'

'We need to pray now,' for the safety of the team and those on the streets.

---

[48] A clicker used to count how many bottles we pick up during each shift.

The team leader has a radio that connects the team to charlie-charlie, the people who monitor CCTV. After brief discussions about the evening ahead and prayer, we leave base for the streets at around 10pm.

'Charlie-charlie, this is Street Pastors checking in.'

'Street Pastors, you are coming through, loud and clear.'

We step out into the sights, sounds and smells of a busy town at night. Young people dressed up and walking around, spilling out of pubs, queuing for clubs, the buzz of conversations, the sounds of traffic, the smells of fast-food outlets.

Our first round lasts until about midnight, before we return to base for a break and a cup of tea or coffee. In the first round, when things are usually quiet, we take the opportunities to chat with the door staff of clubs and pubs. Some door staff will be very familiar with Street Pastors, while ones new to the area may not have met us before.

It's really interesting to meet the door staff, who are from such diverse backgrounds. In general, none of them fulfils the stereotype I had of door staff before I was a Street Pastor, which tended to be a bit negative. Most of the door staff are connected to charlie-charlie by radio. In meeting them, we make them aware that they can call us if they need help with a very drunk or injured person. While sometimes the door staff are too busy to chat as we walk by, in general we get friendly responses from them.

Tonight, at one of the pubs, we meet a young doorman from Afghanistan who, during a brief conversation, tells us, 'I am a Muslim as a way of life, but neither a Sunni nor Shiite. All most of us want in Afghanistan is peace.'

After chatting to the door staff of a few more pubs, we walk past a small club and start chatting to the door staff. The club has just been decorated and one of the door staff asks, 'Would you like to come inside and look around?'

We follow them in and take a quick look round the venue, which at present has no punters, but it is still early. It smells of fresh paint and stale beer. We are surprised how small it is inside.

As we walk past other clubs and pubs, we chat to door staff and young people, giving out a few lollies on the way. Each person we talk to gives us a good reception. This may include high-fives, hugs, compliments or words of encouragement, such as, 'Hi, Street Pasties, I think you do a great job!'

At about 11.30pm, we meet a group of about six people from a local church. They are standing in a pedestrianised area near the centre of town and approaching passers-by. 'Do you fancy a bacon roll and a bottle of water?' they ask us.

'That would be great, thanks.' We stop for a while to eat and chat to them about their role on the streets.

We are now in the centre of town where we generally meet homeless people, presumably because here they have company and might meet people who will give them money or food. Some homeless people will be sleeping rough, on the streets. Others may have somewhere to go, such as someone's sofa.

In this town, in any one night, we can meet up to about ten homeless people. Tonight, the first homeless person we meet is a young man, probably in his twenties or early thirties, who has told us previously that he is a heroin addict.

He is hardly noticed amid the noise of the night, the rushing past of the smartly dressed people out to enjoy themselves; just a small figure of a man in ragged clothes, sitting on a sleeping bag as he leans against a shop window.

'Would you like a coffee?'

'Yes, please, loads of sugar.'

Two of the team wander off to get him a coffee, while the other two stay and chat with him.

'How are you doing? Any chance of getting somewhere to live soon?'

'Not a chance. The council won't offer me a place unless I get clean. They are setting me up to fail.'

'Can we pray for you?'

'Sure; you know, I occasionally go into a Catholic church to pray... I had some Catholic upbringing.'

We pray briefly and generally for him, that he would be safe, be able to come off heroin, and that things would improve for him. Later on, we also phone through to the Prayer Pastors on duty to pray for him.

Before walking back for our break at midnight, we have a few more conversations.

An Iranian man comes up to us and in conversation says, 'You know, I work a twelve-hour day, and never take any money from the state.' Perhaps he was getting a hard time about immigrants being on benefit?

Outside another pub that is spilling both its music and its punters out into the night air, a young woman tells us,

'I think the work that Street Pastors does is great; keep it up. I don't go to church at the moment, but what you do is an inspiration to my faith.'

Around midnight we chat to a homeless man of about thirty-five years old. He asks us, 'Can you tell me a good church to go to? I need some help to get my life a bit sorted.'

We suggest a lively local church.

At the end of town, we talk to a doorman from the north of England, who tells us, 'I am really looking forward to going home at Christmas to spend time with my family.'

As we start to walk back to base for a drink and to warm up, we pass the largest club in town, capable of taking more than 2,000 people. Sometimes outside this club we see queues stretching up to 100 yards; for the most part, keen, eager young faces with optimism for an enjoyable evening. Amid the gathering of young people waiting to go into the club, we see a homeless man sitting on the pavement and ask him, 'Would you like a sandwich?'

'No, thanks, I'm full up,' he replies, 'But have you got any socks?'

'Sorry, no, but we can bring them out in the next round, if you're still here then. Here's a bottle of water for you.'

We get back to base at around 12.30am, and leave to go out again at around 1am for the second round.

Round 2

The pubs are now closed and most people still out are probably in the clubs. The evening at this stage is perceptibly quieter as we walk around town by a similar route to the first round.

The content of the second round depends very much on who and what we meet. On a cold rainy day, it can be really quiet. However, police and door staff sometimes jokingly tell us, 'Don't use the Q word.'

As we are leaving base, we start talking to several people from a local residents' association who are doing a yearly walkabout. During conversation one of them tells us, 'You know, we have a real problem with students walking along some residential roads late at night and in the early hours, making a lot of noise and using people's front gardens as toilets.'

Around 2am near one of the large clubs, we come across a group of about eight people who are mainly homeless, or ex-homeless. None seems particularly drunk; they are just spending time together. At one level they could remind us of individuals from a Dickens novel. All look quite ragged and a little shifty. They become people in their own right as we get to talk to them.

'Would you like some sandwiches?' Soon all the sandwiches are gratefully received.

Among this group, we notice a woman, probably in her late twenties, who has a black eye. Out of concern, one of the team members asks how she got it.

'I was drunk and fell, but I'm going for detox soon.' We wonder if there were other reasons for the black eye, but if there were, she is not letting on.

We stay chatting for a while with different members of the group, before we notice an older man who has started to shake badly. A couple of the team are first aid trained and one is a former nurse, but none of us is a medic. We think the shaking is probably alcohol-related, so decide as an initial response to get him a cup of tea, hoping that might help.

En route to buying the cup of tea, we meet a group of women in their twenties looking glamorous for their night out. They ask us, 'Have you got any flip flops?' as a way of getting out of their heels.

As we open the packs of flip flops and hand them out, they ask in gratitude, 'Can we take your photo?'

We continue on our way when we meet three women in their early twenties and also give them flip flops. Giving out flip flops can momentarily make us feel like angels, based on the appreciation given.

We get back to the man who was shaking, who is now sitting on the ground with some of his friends chatting to him.

'We've got a cup of tea for you,' we say, but by now he is shaking so badly, he can't hold the cup.

If someone is unconscious or badly injured, the decision to call an ambulance is simple. When people are very drunk or otherwise intoxicated, but not unconscious, it is a harder decision, although we learn with experience. This is a more difficult call. As a team we discuss the situation. We don't think the man's condition is life-threatening, but we decide to be on the safe side and call for an ambulance.

As we wait, police arrive and stay with us. One of the officers says, 'It's probably an alcoholic seizure of some sort,' but he also is not sure. The police officer goes on to say, 'We know this guy. He is ex-army, and recently he was given a flat. He invited his homeless friends around who unfortunately caused problems, and he ended up getting thrown out.'

During the wait, we wrap the man lying on the ground with a space blanket and one of the Street Pastors supports his head. It is sad to see someone from an army background, who at one time lived a disciplined life and served his country, reduced to such a state.

The ambulance crew arrives, bustling with care, confidence and professionalism. They ask him and us lots of questions before departing into the night with the man.

Perhaps the scariest ambulance call I have been involved in as a Street Pastor came some years after. One night we came across a woman lying on the pavement. A friend who was on the phone was crouching near.

'Can we help, what's the problem?' we asked.

'It's my friend, she's having an asthma attack. I've phoned for an ambulance.'

Two of the team knelt down beside her as her breathing got more irregular and her body started to convulse. Neither of us was a medic and, as the minutes ticked by and her breathing became more irregular, we were both concerned she was not going to be around by the time the ambulance arrived.

We phoned the ambulance again. 'Is she breathing? What is your location?'

We were relieved to see the ambulance arrive and take over.

Ambulance calls can be categorised from level one to level four, category one being the most urgent for 'a life-threatening condition, such as cardiac or respiratory arrest'; category two being 'a serious condition, such as stroke or chest pain, which may require rapid assessment and/or urgent transport'; category three, 'an urgent problem, such as an uncomplicated diabetic issue, which requires treatment and transport to an acute setting'; and category four, 'a non-urgent problem, such as stable clinical cases, which requires transportation to a hospital ward or clinic'.[49]

Back to the present, and during our wait for the ambulance for the shaking man, the woman with the black eye tells us, 'My boyfriend is being held at the police station for stealing food. Can you take me there so I can stay safe and warm?' We drop her off into the safe and, for her, benevolent care of the police station. As we leave her, a female member of the team prays for her and tells her that God loves her.

As we leave the police station, we respond to a call from charlie-charlie: 'Street Pastors, are you able to assist a very drunk man outside a club?'

We respond in the affirmative. It is now about 3am. We have missed our second break owing to the

[49] North East Ambulance Service NHS, 'Understanding ambulance response categories', https://www.neas.nhs.uk/our-services/accident-emergency/ambulance-response-categories.aspx (accessed 8th July 2020).

ambulance call and can't stop for a break now as we need to attend to the charlie-charlie call.

We reach the club in a few minutes and come across a guy who has been 'celebrating' his eighteenth birthday. He is sitting on the pavement, slumped against a wall in the semi-darkness, looking very dishevelled and unhappy.

'Would you like some water?'

He is almost non-responsive, but manages to take a bottle from us and drink a bit, before being sick.

'Can we help you walk to the bus stop?'

Walking can often help sober people up a bit. Neither buses nor taxis will take really drunk people, who may vomit or cause other problems.

After a while we get the young man, with help from his friend, to the bus stop. His female friend is upset and tearful, and asks, 'Can you stay with us till the bus arrives, please?'

The bus arrives in a few minutes. It is a bit of a struggle to persuade the young man he really needs the bus, but he decides to go for it, and the driver decides to take him.

It is now about 3.30am. It has already felt like a busy evening, with only one break since starting. We are just a few minutes from our base, and possibly packing up for the evening, when a fight erupts about 50ft in front of us. As soon as we see signs of aggression (one guy has taken off his shirt), we radio it into charlie-charlie to monitor, as is our normal practice, hoping it will fizzle out quickly, as such situations often do, before it amounts to anything.

It is like watching in slow motion but being totally helpless to do anything. Several guys are running after each other, and one falls down in the middle of the road, hitting the back of his head, without his fall being broken at all. As he is down, one of the guys chasing him kicks him in the head and runs off. It is over in seconds.

A scrum of about six young people form around the man; it is impossible to know if they are trying to help or not. The ex-nurse in the team manages to push her way through the melee of people to see what help she can offer. His head is bleeding, so we call for the second ambulance of the evening. The police are soon on the scene, taking witness statements, including from some of the Street Pastors. Soon, plain-clothes CID are also on the scene, talking to those milling around, and the entire area is cordoned off.

The injured man is still in the middle of the road. It takes about forty minutes for the ambulance to arrive. During this time the ex-nurse Street Pastor has bandaged his head wound and keeps him in the recovery position, with his head supported. He remains semiconscious and is sick before the ambulance arrives.

At about 4.15am, our evening comes to an end. A new Street Pastor from another area who has come out with us that evening tells us, 'That's an evening I won't forget for a while.'

Chapter 4
Stories from Greater London

Covering an area of 620 square miles, Greater London is made up of thirty-two boroughs, and Street Pastors operates in all but two of them. With a population of some seven million, boosted by millions of commuters and visitors, it is a teeming, thriving and cosmopolitan area.

Working on the streets of Greater London, Street Pastors meet a diverse range of people from all over the world. They also address a wide range of needs, from supporting and befriending rough sleepers, helping young people who are stranded or so intoxicated that they cannot function alone, talking to people with mental health issues, to discouraging and de-escalating conflict.

In a densely populated area like London, crime statistics are correspondingly high. For example, in February 2020 the Metropolitan police recorded 16,975 antisocial behaviour incidents, 6,216 burglaries and 17,959 violent crimes. In total they recorded 86,984 crimes.[50]

---

[50] UK Crime Stats,
https://ukcrimestats.com/Police_Force/Metropolitan_Police_Service
(accessed 3rd July 2020).

Homelessness is also a growing problem in Greater London, with people moving there from other parts of the country, swelling the existing numbers. Outreach workers reported 8,855 people who were seen sleeping rough in London during 2018/19, an 18 per cent increase on numbers seen in 2017/18.[51] This number is two and a half times the number seen ten years earlier in 2008/09.

The following stories are related by different experienced Street Pastors from Greater London and illustrate how Street Pastors have intervened in urban settings. Some stories could have had a different outcome, becoming a personal tragedy, a sad crime statistic or a disturbing newspaper headline.

Sylvia, now in her seventies, recounts some unforgettable stories, including those of people who nearly lost their lives on the busy streets of their London borough town.

A near-death experience
Standing outside one of the clubs, we watched people running across the busy town centre road, dodging the traffic. Suddenly a large lorry passed by. A young man was standing on the roof of the lorry pretending to windsurf. As the lorry swung around the corner he was catapulted onto the road, where he lay face down.

Door staff from the nightclub ran into the road to keep him still. We raced into the road with our backs to the traffic so our reflector vests could warn motorists to

---

[51] London Datastore, 'Rough Sleeping in London (Chain Reports)', https://data.london.gov.uk/dataset/chain-reports (accessed 3rd July 2020).

avoid the spot. It was a miracle he survived the fall and wasn't hit by the speeding traffic.

The nightclub paramedic thought he had sustained a broken cheekbone and serious lacerations to his ear and face. The young man was so drunk he had no idea what had happened. When told that he had fallen off the top of a lorry, his only response was, 'Cool.' Perhaps because he was so drunk when he fell, he was very limp and relaxed so his injuries were not as bad as they might have been. God was looking after him that night.

Life saving
It was a very rainy, cold night, so cold everyone had gone home early and so wet that the rain was gushing off the peak of my cap like a waterfall. It was 3am, and as we walked back to our base, we passed a stack of black sacks put out for the street cleaner. Three of the team looked and walked on by but the last person noticed something odd and went across to see what it was.

He found a young man collapsed behind the rubbish bags who was only wearing trousers, a shirt and a pair of trainers. It was a miracle he spotted him. Unconscious and freezing cold, the man was unresponsive to our calls and touch. All four of us carried him to the nearest bench, wrapped him in a space blanket and one of us folded our arms around to keep him warm until an ambulance arrived. He was sick four times without regaining consciousness.

When the paramedics arrived, they took one look at him and loaded him into the ambulance. By this time his mobile had rung and we were able to tell his friends they would find him at the local hospital.

He was so blessed that one of us had seen him, as he was so well hidden. We probably saved his life, which made being soaked to the skin worthwhile. I still have nightmares about what would have happened if we had walked on.

Bus riot

One night we were expecting to finish early when we heard an alarm go off. Following the noise, we came across a night bus with its lights flashing and alarm ringing. Several people had stormed onto the bus and gone upstairs without paying and were making a lot of noise, pounding the floor. Others were trying to get on and the driver was in his cab waiting for a response to his alarm.

We tried to calm the driver down and pleaded with the passengers to 'give him a break'. Some new arrivals wanted to enter the bus and started kicking the front doors, which would not close properly, so the driver couldn't move off even if he wanted to. We radioed for the police, but they were busy elsewhere. Another bus sent to take the passengers off drove away when the driver saw the commotion. It was chaos!

We gathered together to pray for the driver and passengers. When the driver tried the door once more, it opened and closed properly. Thanks be to God.

The poor driver was a complete wreck but managed to pull away. This all lasted about an hour. We stopped to pray again for him to have a safe journey as none of us felt he was in a fit state to drive after that.

Street sleeper robbed

We came across a rough sleeper, aged twenty-seven, who had been 'rolled' by youngsters who had stolen his shoes and £3.50, all the money he had. We took him back to our church base where we found him clean socks, a better sleeping bag and a nearly new pair of size nine walking boots that fitted better than Cinderella's slippers. We also gave him some food and a hot drink. A new observer who was out with us that night was totally blown away.

Young people often start out their night 'on the town' with friends, but for one reason or another become separated from them. A Street Pastors team leader describes one such event.

Twin trouble

During our round one winter's evening, we received a radio call to attend a distressed woman at a nearby taxi rank. She was trying to persuade the driver of a black cab to take her watch as security so he would drive her to her boyfriend's house, twelve miles away, where she promised he would collect his fare. The negotiations were going nowhere. We found her sobbing on a bench, and approached her to ask if we could help.

She told us she'd been evicted from a nightclub for being drunk and was without her purse, phone, bag or coat. With mascara running down her cheek she said she'd come out with her twin sister, Marilyn, and friends to celebrate their twenty-first birthday but now had no way of contacting anyone and no way of getting home, and was very cold.

We decided to return to the nightclub with her and talk to the door staff about contacting her identical twin and friends still inside. On explaining the situation, the staff informed us that it would be impossible to find or relay a message to the party as their four dance floors had a total of 3,000 people in that night.

Somewhat dismayed, we regrouped to figure out Plan B, when the woman asked to use the club's toilet. We asked a female member of the door staff to accompany her while we waited outside by the entrance. As we waited, we prayed for a solution.

Within minutes there appeared our damsel in distress, this time immaculate with a chic hairstyle and perfect make-up. After our double take, we quickly twigged that this must be her twin sister and we cried out in desperate unison, 'Marilyn!'

Shocked, Marilyn turned towards us and we beckoned her over to tell her we had found her sister. She said she'd spent the last half hour searching for her and was becoming very worried. As if on cue, her very bedraggled twin reappeared with the female member of the door staff and started haranguing her sister for not looking out for her. All were safely, if not happily, reunited.

After Sally, in her seventies, heard that when Street Pastors patrol her local town centre there are fewer crimes and fewer people attend A&E, she decided to become one.

My early experiences were excellent because of the teams I went out with. One of the leaders had great discernment about where to go and when. For example, we might be walking down a street when she would suggest we turn down a dark alley. I would look at it and think, 'What's the point? It's deserted and has a dead end,' but near the end we would come across someone in trouble, like a woman crying in a doorway.

Predatory

We were about to finish a patrol when we came across a woman sitting on a low wall, clearly drunk. A young man was standing protectively over her. I thought, 'No need to worry about her, the young man will make sure she gets home safely.' We asked if she was OK, and she replied that she was, but the more experienced members of the team sensed immediately that the woman did not know the young man. The young man claimed he had found her wandering and lost. However, we worked out that she lived in the opposite direction to the one in which he had been taking her. The team helped the woman phone the friend she had been with earlier in the evening, who came to fetch her.

No memory

One night we came across a young man sitting on a wall. He told us he had permission from his girlfriend, who was away at the time, to spend the night at her flat.

However, he had drunk so much that he couldn't remember her address or the code to get into his mobile phone to look it up. One of the Street Pastors realised that the phone had fingerprint recognition, so he helped him to unlock his phone and find the address. The young man let us walk with him to the flat.

'This is very embarrassing,' he said on the way there.

'Why?' I asked.

'Because I'm not a Christian.'

We assured him that it did not matter whether he was a Christian, a member of another religion or an atheist, we would still help him.

City gent

Once we came across a young man in a pinstripe suit curled up and asleep on the pavement, in a corner. We woke him up and asked if he would like to be taken to a place of safety. He groggily shook his head and slurred, 'No', then collapsed back to sleep. We walked on. During the patrol a grateful café manager gave us some curry, thankful we were making a significant difference to the area. On our way back we woke the sleeping man.

'Will you let us take you to a safe place?'

'No,' he slurred.

'We've got a curry. Would you like some?' we asked.

'Yeah,' he replied, more enthusiastically. So this time we helped him up and took him to the night shelter, where he promptly fell fast asleep. In the end we ate the curry, which was delicious.

Stop the fight

An off-duty nurse went to help a young woman who had collapsed on the pavement. Her boyfriend and the boyfriend of her female companion disagreed about whether the nurse should help or not, and they came to blows. They were fighting close to the two women.

I moved over to stand between the men and women. One of the men gave the other such a wallop that he fell over backwards on top of me. Fortunately, I was wearing many layers of clothes so was completely unharmed, and anyway, it stopped the fight.

Our uniform and caps seem to help bring people to their senses, at least long enough to stop some rivals being aggressive. Once a shouting match started by a man, which could have resulted in violence, ended with hugs all round – the ideal way of finishing any disagreement.

Over the years I have only seen relatively few aggressive incidents. Some door staff have told me that since the Street Pastors started patrolling in the town the incidence of fighting has decreased dramatically.

We were not in time to halt one recent scrap, though. In the distance we saw two women chasing a young man across the road, and kicking him, which they continued to do even when he fell. As we approached, the women ran off. Luckily, the man had a doctor friend who helped him up and mopped the blood, which was flowing freely. We were shocked, as it was the first time we had seen women acting so aggressively. It transpired that the women had been thrown out of a pub for being unruly and the young man had been trying to calm them down.

We were told that there is a drug on the market which, when mixed with alcohol, makes people feel very angry for no reason.

Near-accident

In one area that we patrol the clientele tends to be young adults with well-paid jobs and good prospects, but that does not stop them overdoing it. On one occasion a young woman walked into the road without looking and a driver had to perform an emergency stop to avoid hitting her. She then leaned right over the bonnet of his car and seemed to fall asleep. The traffic was piling up behind, so the driver honked his horn to get her to move, whereupon she walked deliberately to the side of his car and snapped off his wing mirror – which made him swear at her.

We escorted her to the nearby Hub, a local church, where she could sit quietly and calm down. When we returned a couple of hours later, she was ranting and raving and threatening to report the driver to the police for swearing at her. I don't expect she remembers it at all.

Carrie has been a Street Pastor since 2007 when she was a member of the first team to patrol the streets of her busy local town centre in south London. She describes her favourite experience, which involves university students.

'Amazing Grace'

We started chatting to a group of women, students training to become nurses, all in their early twenties. They wanted to know about Street Pastors because one of them had an uncle who was a pastor in a Pentecostal church.

We explained who we were and what we do and they told us that they enjoyed being in a choir. They then burst into an impromptu rendition of 'Amazing Grace'. This soon attracted a small crowd, including a group of young men.

At the time, the song 'Amazing Grace' was in the news as a film with the exact same name, about the abolition of slavery and the work of William Wilberforce, was circulating in the cinemas. This led to a thoughtful conversation about how faith can transform lives. It felt like a very special spiritual time as we all joined together in the singing.

Last word from a rough sleeper

Some years ago, I was homeless and destitute, living on the streets of Harrow in north London. I had come from Europe looking for work but found none. One cold November night a local shop owner called over some Street Pastors and told me, 'These people will help you.'

I couldn't speak much English then but I did tell them my name. They gave me some food and drink. They couldn't give me a place to stay but they told me how to find a homeless charity. The charity offered me a place in a night shelter which was going to open in January, two months later.

In the meantime, I slept on the stairs of a car park. I had a sleeping bag and some blankets. The Street Pastors gave me tissues and water so I managed to keep clean.

Eventually I was housed and given help to learn English and support to find a job.

Three years later I recognised one of those Street Pastors who had been on that team. I was so happy to be able to thank him and tell him how much better my life was as a result of meeting them.

These personal stories are just a small snapshot of the tremendous impact Street Pastors are making on the streets of our capital city. Street Pastors have come a long way since they first began patrolling Brixton in the London borough of Lambeth in April 2003. From Lambeth it spread quickly to neighbouring Hackney, then in 2004 to a third London borough, Lewisham, followed by Kingston. In less than two years Street Pastors had been established in two other major cities, Birmingham and Manchester, the rapid expansion of the work illustrating how much God cares about our cities.

Chapter 5
Street Pastors and the Homeless

Most of us who live in towns or cities across the UK will see people on the streets who are begging, possibly homeless and sleeping rough. No doubt this leads to us each reacting in different ways, depending on our experiences and understanding of homelessness and homeless people.

One of the many causes leading to people becoming homeless is domestic violence, which can cause people, particularly women, LGBT people and young persons, to leave home to escape the perpetrator. Despite the vulnerability of such people, apparently an increasing number are finding it difficult to get accommodation.[52]

Affordability is another significant driver of homelessness among single people, and this is also increasingly affecting older people with modest incomes in London.[53]

---

[52] London Assembly Housing Committee, 'Hidden homelessness in London',
https://www.london.gov.uk/sites/default/files/london_assembly_-_hidden_homelessness_report.pdf (accessed 8th July 2020).
[53] Ibid.

'Sofa surfing' is an initial option for some people who are made homeless. However, this can lead to poor mental health associated with the energy of trying to find accommodation each night and the nomadic experience of it all.[54] When the kindness of friends and family runs out, those sofa surfing can become increasingly desperate, and finally end up on the streets.[55]

Living on the streets must be really tough. To make things worse, recent research shows that almost 80 per cent of rough sleepers have suffered some sort of violence, abuse or antisocial behaviour in the past year: 48 per cent reported being intimidated or threatened, 35 per cent reported being kicked or other physical violence, 9 per cent reported being urinated on and 7 per cent reported sexual assault.[56]

Street Pastors is not a charity set up to tackle the huge problems of homelessness that currently exist in the UK. However, its core aim is 'caring, listening and helping', as mentioned before. At an individual level, Street Pastors can come across homeless people, some of whom are sleeping rough. During some evenings, depending on the location, time of year and more, it may be that the majority of the interactions of a team could be with homeless people.

Adam, a man in his twenties, was on the streets for about eighteen months. While his story is unique, it no

---

[54] Ibid.

[55] Ibid.

[56] Crisis, 'New research reveals the scale of violence against rough sleepers', https://www.crisis.org.uk/about-us/latest-news/new-research-reveals-the-scale-of-violence-against-rough-sleepers/ (accessed 8th July 2020).

doubt contains elements that are common to many people who are on the streets. To help us understand more about some of the issues that people on the streets go through, Adam here kindly shares the story of his upbringing, which contributed to his homelessness, and a bit about life on the streets.

While this is not specifically a Street Pastors story, Adam was helped by a Christian homelessness charity to which Street Pastors refers individuals.

Adam tells us:

I don't know much about my father, but I know that my parents married while he was in Wormwood Scrubs prison. He walked out when I was hospitalised, having my right kidney taken out in Great Ormond Street Hospital, when I was about six months old.

My mother suffers from borderline personality disorder, which made her volatile and prone to paranoid delusions and violent outbursts. This was exacerbated by her alcoholism and addiction to benzodiazepines. I have a half-brother that I've met once, but he was taken into care before I was born, so it was only ever my mum and myself growing up.

I was taught to lie pretty early on, especially to anyone in Social Services or similar professions. I have plenty of instances of my mum's extreme behaviour, but I guess the one that stands out for me was when I was eight years old and she pinned me against the wall with a kitchen knife to my throat, screaming that she was going to kill me. Suicide attempts were frequent and used as a threat in order to exert some kind of control.

I found alcohol pretty early in life and would drink to blackout almost every time I picked up.[57] My behaviour would often change in this state and I wouldn't recognise the person who would often be described back to me by friends or partners.

The one thing my mum did instil in me was the importance of school, and even though I didn't put in the work that others did, I managed to get decent grades, enough to find a job in data entry.

IT and maths came naturally to me, so finding employment that involved working with search engine advertising was fortunate, but also a very good fit for me.

I managed to get some independence through work, but my drinking and drug use would always bleed into it, and eventually I would have to leave the job or be fired. I used cocaine to try to stop the blackouts, but it just led to longer using periods and more depression. I would go in two-year cycles of finding a job, getting promoted, becoming complacent, losing the job and then having to walk away from my accommodation. I would go back and stay with my mum, but the relationship would break down very quickly, because of her illness and my resentments.

In 2015, I had reached the end of another cycle, but this also coincided with my mother's antipsychotic medication being changed after almost fifteen years. When I moved back in with her, her delusions got

---

[57] 'Picked up': started drinking.

worse and her paranoia towards me reached new heights. Without any other family to turn to, I ran out of sofas to sleep on and ended up turning to a local Christian charity that works with the homeless, helping them, if possible, to find accommodation. Owing to my behaviour, I was not able to maintain a place in the local night shelter, and ended up sleeping rough for about eighteen months.

Starting out on the streets was a very difficult adjustment for me. I would spend my days walking around the streets I grew up on and often past the houses of people I had once considered friends. You learn a lot about yourself and those you've had around you when you lose everything. I fell into a very dark depression and sought assistance from every service available. Because of my drinking there were no options available to me, and I wasn't ready to admit I had a problem. Not being able to manage the benefits I received meant that I needed to find another source to ease my worsening physical dependence on alcohol.

I started shoplifting. I found a similar group of homeless alcoholics and we spent our days going from town to town stealing from supermarkets, then finding a suitably isolated spot to spend the night. Eventually we found a disused house and began squatting. We had electricity, but no running water and no windows. This meant that it got very cold in the winter months, but it was away from people, which meant that we were less in a constant state of alert. This was also helped by the fact that the building was surrounded by a high wooden fence, so we would hear if anyone were to climb over it.

The police were called many times because passers-by would see us climb the fence, but they would stand outside and shine their torches through the 'windows', not wanting to come in owing to the unhealthy conditions we were living in. Being arrested actually provided some respite, as you'd have hot meals and the doctor would provide regular diazepam to stave off alcoholic seizures.

Along with the arrests, there was fighting, drug use, and the worst of all was seeing people you used to know, in your dishevelled state. It could be weeks without a shower. I would shoplift expensive clothes to try to tell myself that things hadn't got too bad. However, during this period of eighteen months, I was admitted to three different psychiatric wards, attempted suicide more than once, moved on to crack and heroin and gained multiple convictions for a number of offences.

It was only when I lost a few friends owing to addiction that I started realising that I could not sustain this lifestyle. I had to make changes, and the first was alcohol and drugs. I begged, pleaded and even slept outside the office of the local Christian homelessness charity for a few weeks, before I got in to rehab.

After what felt like a lifetime, I was offered a place in rehab, but the process was not quick. I came very close to going to prison. If it had not been for the people who worked for the Christian homelessness charity that I had contacted before, I would have surely not have been able to turn things around.

I used my last substance on 21st June 2016 and have been clean ever since. I've done a lot of work on myself in that time but am aware that I could throw it all away with one bad decision. Today, I am holding down a full-time job in my previous career and perform at a much higher level than I have ever done before. I'm not sure why, but I have distanced myself from fellowships like AA [Alcoholics Anonymous]; however, taking one day at a time seems to be working for me – today.

It's been a difficult journey, but I don't think I'd still be sober if it hadn't been for those experiences. Whenever I feel like a drink, I think back to those suicidal feelings and realise I never want to be there again.

Having heard Adam's moving story, what are some more of the factors that lead to people being on the streets? How can members of the public help and how do Street Pastors help?

The charity Shelter, which was founded in 1996 and plans to end homelessness and bad housing in England and Scotland, stated that 320,000 people were recorded as homeless in Britain in 2018.[58] This represents a rise of 13,000 people who were homeless, or a 4 per cent rise compared to 2017 figures, and is equivalent to thirty-six new people becoming homeless every day.[59]

Of those 320,000 homeless people, the estimated number of people actually sleeping rough rose from

---

[58] Shelter, '320,000 People in Britain are now homeless, as numbers keep rising', https://england.shelter.org.uk/media/press_releases/articles/320,00 0_people_in_britain_are_now_homeless,_as_numbers_keep_rising (accessed 8th July 2020).
[59] Ibid.

1,768 in 2010 to 4,751 in 2017, a rise of almost three times.[60] However, a different estimation puts the number of people sleeping rough as 8,108 people in London alone during 2016/17, similar to the estimate of 8,096 people seen in 2015/16.[61]

A Crisis charity spokesman said, 'Not everyone who begs is homeless and not all homeless people will beg. Nevertheless, people who do beg are often some of the most vulnerable in our society, and many will be struggling with extreme poverty.'[62]

The advice regarding what to give to someone who is begging and possibly sleeping rough varies. Thames Reach, a London-based charity that supports the homeless, advised that giving money to beggars 'can have fatal consequences'.[63] This is because some beggars may be hard drug users, and there is a possibility of a fatal dose from, for example, overdosing on heroin.[64]

The Salvation Army, a charity well known for its work with the homeless, also advises against handing money to homeless people, saying, 'It risks "trapping" people in

[60] Homeless link, https://www.homeless.org.uk (accessed 8th July 2020).
[61] London Assembly Housing Committee, 'Hidden homelessness in London', https://www.london.gov.uk/sites/default/files/london_assembly_-_hidden_homelessness_report.pdf (accessed 10th September 2020).
[62] Cherry Wilson, 'Should we give money to beggars?' BBC News, 28th September 2016, https://www.bbc.co.uk/news/uk-37492659 (accessed 8th July 2020).
[63] Ibid.
[64] Robert C Oelhaf and Mohammadreza Azadfard, 'Heroin Toxicity', StatPearls Publishing LLC, 2020, https://www.ncbi.nlm.nih.gov/books/NBK430736/ (accessed 8th July 2020).

the "endless cycle" of homelessness and rough sleeping.'[65]

However, there are mixed views among charities and support groups for the homeless. Some groups say that homeless people need money for bare essentials.[66]

Generally accepted items to give to homeless people include water, food that can be eaten without cutlery, new socks, gloves and underwear, hotel-sized toiletries, clean second-hand clothes (but not new, expensive clothes that may be sold or stolen), blankets and sleeping bags.[67]

Factors that may play a role in someone being homeless can include a lack of qualifications, relationship breakdown or substance abuse, as well as family background issues such as disputes, sexual and physical abuse from parents or guardians, or a previous experience of family homelessness.[68] Sometimes the issues leading to homelessness come from outside an individual's control, such as lack of support for those leaving care, the armed forces or prison, leading to life on the streets.[69]

---

[65] Mark Bullman, 'Should We Give Homeless People Money?' *The Independent*, 10th January 2018, https://www.independent.co.uk/news/uk/home-news/should-we-give-homeless-money-a8124951.html (accessed 8th July 2020

[66] Ibid.

[67] Jeremy Myers, '10 Dos and Don'ts in Loving Homeless People', Redeeming God, https://redeeminggod.com/10-dos-and-donts-in-loving-homeless-people/ (accessed 8th July 2020).

[68] Ibid.

[69] Ibid.

The causes leading to individuals becoming homeless are numerous.[70] Between 2016 and 2017, these included factors such as parents no longer able to or willing to provide accommodation for their children (8,520 households); domestic violence (6,580 households); nonviolent relationship breakdowns (2,900 households) and mortgage or rent arrears (360 households).[71]

However, the main cause of homelessness during this time, accounting for a massive 31 per cent of cases (18,750 households), was loss of a private tenancy, with nowhere to go after eviction.[72]

The ways in which Street Pastors interact with and support the homeless varies from area to area. Just a few examples are given here.

Street Pastors teams in Glasgow, on any given weekend, will hold at least fifty conversations with people on the streets who are homeless and often sleeping rough, and they will give out a similar number of hats, gloves, socks, underwear, etc.

Possibly more than practical help, time spent listening and engaging with people is appreciated. One young man commented, 'Street Pastors helped me to feel that I mattered as a human being, when thousands walked past during the day, not even noticing I was there.'

Glasgow Street Pastors have close links with other agencies working to support the homeless, especially the

---

[70] L Geraghty, 'What is the main cause of homelessness?', *The Big Issue*, 6th April 2018, https://www.bigissue.com/latest/what-is-the-main-cause-of-homelessness/ (accessed 8th July 2020).
[71] Ibid.
[72] Ibid.

City Mission. On a Friday night it runs a 'Safe Zone'. This is a place where people can drop in for tea/coffee, toast and some conversation and company. This is often used by homeless people.

From December to March in Glasgow, the City Mission runs an emergency night shelter for the homeless. Street Pastors will either walk with or arrange a taxi to take people to the venue as needed.

Also in Glasgow, Street Pastors teams carry booklets with information to signpost homeless people and rough sleepers to other agencies and services. These are particularly helpful for people who are new to the city, although the homeless 'community' share information and look out for each other, pointing to places where food, clothing and shelter can be found.

In Plymouth, Street Pastors usually interact with about ten to fifteen homeless people each night they are out. These people tend to be mainly men from about seventeen years old to late fifties.

To provide assistance to the homeless, the team carries hats, gloves, scarves and vouchers given by a local café to get food. The team also supplies information on where to access free food. Some of the Street Pastors carry chocolate bars to hand out.

For further help in Plymouth, Street Pastors signposts individuals to a local charity that has been running since 1990 and offers a comprehensive range of services for people. These services include support with housing, drug and alcohol advice, benefits advice, training, education, employment or just a listening ear.

An ex-homeless man from this area said the main thing he appreciated was, 'Basic respect, such as people looking us in the eye and using our name. Also, people who care enough to spend some time with us and listen.' This man went on to say, 'These things alone made me feel that there was light at the end of the tunnel after being kicked and spat on for being on the streets.'

In Kingston, Street Pastors typically come across between one and ten homeless people each night they are out. These people are mainly men, but probably about 10 per cent or so are women.

Kingston Street Pastors operates in a similar way to Street Pastors in Glasgow and Plymouth, but gives out food rather than vouchers. In addition to giving out food, the team gives out clothes, sleeping bags and packs as available that contain items such as soap, toothpaste and underwear, and spend time in conversation.

Street Pastors teams in Kingston also signpost individuals to relevant local charities, such as the Joel Community night shelter,[73] Kingston Churches Action on Homelessness[74] and places that may provide meals for the homeless.

In Kingston, an ex-army man who was rough sleeping said, 'Without you guys, we could not survive.'

Probably all Street Pastors teams that encounter the homeless work in similar ways to those described for Glasgow, Plymouth and Kingston.

---

[73] The Joel Community, https://www.joelcommunity.org (accessed 16th July 2020).

[74] Kingston Churches Action on Homelessness, https://www.kcah.org.uk (accessed 16th July 2020).

Street Pastors offer prayer to homeless people if it is felt appropriate, as they would for others. Such offers of prayer are rarely refused, and usually are received with thanks.

Here is a poignant story about prayer:

I was out the other Saturday night when we came across a rough sleeper, usually a reasonably cheerful man. That night he was quiet, low, subdued. As I listened to him, he told me he felt there was no future, no hope. I offered to pray with him. He readily accepted my suggestion.

So, as sometimes happens, I found myself holding the hands of the man, amid all that rubbish and debris of disregarded burger wrappers and beer cans, while the noise of city night life sounded all around. Yet all seemed so quiet, so peaceful and still to me. What prayers can be voiced for a man who has nothing except the contents of a carrier bag and who feels he has no hope, no joy, no happiness, no future, no safety?

So I prayed that our Father would give him somewhere safe for the night where he would be sheltered, where he could find some peace and some happiness in his future.

When the prayers were finished the man turned to me and said he didn't know if he would ever find peace and happiness while he was alive, but he had suddenly realised that there was a future where there would be peace and safety, where he would be loved, perhaps not on this earth, but in another world, eternity. He realised there was something more than this life on earth.

Chapter 6
A Desperate Call for Help

In 2018, there were 6,507 registered deaths by suicide in the UK.[75] This equates to about eighteen deaths per day and is significantly higher than 2017.[76] Males of forty-five to fifty years old have the highest age-specific suicide rate, but for under twenty-fives, the rates have increased in recent years, and this difference was significant for ten- to twenty-five-year-old females.[77]

In October 2018, the then Prime Minister, Theresa May, pledged more funding for the charity Samaritans,[78] which provides a free twenty-four-hour helpline for those people who may be contemplating suicide. Theresa May also announced the UK''s first Minister for Suicide Prevention.[79]

---

[75] Office for National Statistics, 'Suicides in the UK: 2018 registrations', https://www.ons.gov.uk/peoplepopulationandcommunity/birthsdeathsandmarriages/deaths/bulletins/suicidesintheunitedkingdom/2018registrations (accessed 8th July 2020).
[76] Ibid.
[77] Ibid.
[78] GOV.UK, 'PM pledges action on suicide to mark World Mental Health Day', https://www.gov.uk/government/news/pm-pledges-action-on-suicide-to-mark-world-mental-health-day (accessed 8th July 2020).
[79] Ibid.

With respect to the homeless population, which Street Pastors encounter on a regular basis, they are reported to be at particular risk from suicide, owing to multiple complex issues that relate to social exclusion, alcohol, drug, mental health and nutritional issues.[80] In one study, where 330 homeless adults were interviewed, 28 per cent of the men and 57 per cent of the women had attempted suicide.[81]

On occasions, Street Pastors may encounter individuals who appear depressed, or verbalise that they are considering suicide. In such circumstances we exercise our listening skills, show care and try to help. The help that can be offered on the streets at night may be limited to listening and signposting the individuals to a suitable organisation such as Samaritans.

However, at a more urgent level, Street Pastors in some locations may occasionally get called to talk to people on the streets who are threatening suicide, or on occasions may have taken an overdose.

While the initial Street Pastors training does not always include suicide prevention training, groups around the country may arrange their own specific training.

For example, in Kingston, the council's public health team regularly offers two-day mental health first aid

---

[80] A Bonner and C Luscombe, 'Suicide and homelessness', *Journal of Public Mental Health*, Volume 8, Issue 3, 2009, pp 7-19, https://doi.org/10.1108/17465729200900016 (accessed 8th July 2020).
[81] R I Eynan, J Langley, G Tolomiczenko et al, 'The Association Between Homelessness and Suicidal Ideation and Behaviors: Results of a Cross-Sectional Survey', *Suicide and Life-Threatening Behavior*, Volume 32, Issue 4, 2002, pp 418-27.

(MHFA) courses. These courses are made available to Street Pastors free of charge. About 20 per cent of the active Street Pastors volunteers in Kingston have achieved certification as Mental Health First Aiders. The aim for Kingston is to get all Street Pastors trained in MHFA.

Also in Kingston, additional training days have included talks from Samaritans, and some of the Street Pastors have attended a suicide prevention training course called SafeTALK.[82]

In Edinburgh, for the last three years the city council has offered Street Pastors a two-day suicide prevention training course called ASIST[83] that several of the team have done and rate very highly. The course looks at identifying people at risk, engaging at an early stage and intervention advice, plus signposting to professional organisations.

In Glasgow, during the past year volunteers have completed the SafeTALK suicide awareness course (as per Kingston) delivered by Social Services. A significant number have also completed the ASIST course (as per Edinburgh). Also in Glasgow, for new recruits, a session in the training programme under the safeguarding of vulnerable people includes suicide awareness.

In Taunton the county council offers Street Pastors free MHFA training (undertaken over two days), and a number of the team have chosen to do this. Additionally,

---

[82] Grassroots, safeTALK: Suicide Alertness For Everyone, https://www.prevent-suicide.org.uk/training-courses/safetalk-suicide-alertness/ (accessed 8th July 2020).
[83] Applied Suicide Intervention Skills Training.

Avon and Somerset Constabulary have in the past given Street Pastors in Taunton a leaflet entitled 'Crisis Intervention and Potential Suicide Avoidance – voluntary sector', which has been used as part of training. This leaflet comments that most people who feel suicidal don't want to die, but they don't want to live their lives as they are. Although this may seem a small difference, it is a vital distinction and a reason why talking with people who feel suicidal is so important.

On its website, Samaritans lists a number of factors that may contribute to people feeling suicidal, such as relationship problems, bereavement, financial worries and job stress, college or study-related stress, loneliness, depression or other mental health issues, heavy use of drugs or alcohol and more.[84]

The charity MIND also offers advice and information about supporting individuals who may be suicidal or may have attempted suicide, with a free online booklet. This booklet suggests phoning 999 or 111 for NHS Direct for more extreme situations, and then staying with the person until the ambulance arrives.[85]

Here we focus on a few incidents in which teams have been involved with those threatening suicide, or with someone who had taken an overdose, but this excludes the work of Rail Pastors.

---

[84] Samaritans, https://www.samaritans.org/how-we-can-help/if-youre-worried-about-someone-else/how-support-someone-youre-worried-about/ (accessed 10th September 2020).
[85] Mind, 'Supporting someone who feels suicidal', https://www.mind.org.uk/information-support/helping-someone-else/supporting-someone-who-feels-suicidal/about-suicidal-feelings/ (accessed 8th July 2020).

A man on a bridge

In one threatened suicide, the police called the local Street Pastors team to talk to a man standing on the edge of bridge, threatening to jump.

One of the Street Pastors on duty that night recounts the story:

The team leader got a call on charlie-charlie asking us to talk to a man standing on a bridge and threatening suicide. As we approached the scene, we saw the police near their patrol car, but some distance from a bare-chested man. The man looked like he was in his twenties and was probably the worse for a number of drinks.

He looked distraught as he clung to the bridge parapet. The water was about 25ft below. While a fall itself may not have been fatal, being in a deep and fast-flowing river in his state of mind may well have been.

We were advised that the man had told the police, 'If you come near me, I'll jump.' His concerns related specifically to the police approaching him, and as such, [there was a] call to Street Pastors to talk to him.

The police went on to advise the team that the man 'had been in a fight, and fallen out with a number of people'.

The team leader for the night approached carefully and started to talk to the man. I had only been a Street Pastor for a few months at that stage, and was glad that I was not the one doing the talking.

As the team leader started to talk to the man, the police drove off. The rest of the team stood some distance away to give them some space, praying for a good outcome.

I couldn't hear what was being said, but body language suggested the tension was slowly easing.

After about ten minutes or so, it was a huge relief when the man distanced himself from the bridge parapet.

As he walked away from the bridge with the team, he asked us, 'Would you wait with me, please, till my bus arrives?' He seemed concerned about the people he had had a fight with, in case they might still be around.

We waited for ten minutes or so until his bus arrived, and said goodbye to a smiling and grateful man as he stepped on board the bus.

Two people climbing the parapet of a bridge
Another bridge incident and a Street Pastor who was present takes up the story:

One night out, the team came across two young people who came up to us and were keen to talk. Quite quickly in conversation it became apparent that they probably had mental health issues. They started telling us they were planning to jump off a building. While they did not seem in earnest, it was not clear that they were joking either.

One of them then told us clearly that they had mental health issues and had been sectioned but had somehow got out for the night.

We were concerned, but at this stage were not sure what, if anything, we could do to help. We stayed chatting and walked with them for a while.

The situation grew more critical as they walked to a small bridge over a river, and then they started chatting to each other about jumping off.

'Let's jump together,' one of them suggested. The stakes got higher as they started climbing up the bridge parapet, probably just for attention, but we had no way of knowing for sure.

A couple of the team grabbed hold of them and held them back. The potential jumpers remained calm; as such, the team members themselves were not in danger. Meanwhile, the team leader told one of the team to 'get the police as quickly as possible'.

Luckily a police station was nearby. The police were soon on the scene and a mental health emergency response team was called for.

It ended as well as it could have done, with no one harmed. The mental health emergency response team were on the scene quite quickly and took over looking after these two vulnerable young people.

As we walked off into the rest of the night, we hoped and prayed that the mental health of these two young people would improve.

Distraught woman

In a non-bridge incident, one night a team came across a young woman walking round the centre of a busy town in the early hours of the morning in pyjamas. She was wearing a hospital blanket as a shawl.

'The hospital has discharged me onto the streets,' she told us. 'If I don't get back to hospital, I'm going to commit suicide.'

The team spent time with her to see if there was any other way to help her. In talking to her it became clear that she had significant mental health issues and really wanted to be taken to hospital. It was the only solution for her in the circumstances.

The team phoned 999 and waited with her on the crowded, busy streets for an ambulance to arrive. For other reasons, a rapid response ambulance car and an ambulance arrived on the scene, but neither was able to take her. We were told the ambulance services were really hard pressed and, because of the mental health issues of the woman, the rapid response ambulance car would not take her alone.

After an hour or so, the team saw the woman safely taken into a different ambulance. The woman stayed chatty for most of the waiting time, and thanked us for staying with her.

River jump

A team leader tells of one night she was on patrol when a young woman jumped into a river:

> We heard on charlie-charlie that 'a young woman has jumped in the river', so I instructed the team to quickly make their way to the location. As we walked there, I phoned through to our Prayer Pastors on duty, to pray for the safety of the woman.
>
> When we arrived, we found that two of the door staff from a nearby club and two members of the public had pulled a young woman from the river.
>
> As a team we wrapped the woman in three space blankets, before the police arrived on the scene.

One of the police officers asked her, 'Did you fall in the river, or jump?'

'I jumped,' she replied.

The police managed to contact her family. She did not want to talk to her mum, and became really distressed and upset when talking to her dad.

Finally, a positive outcome, her dad agreed to come and collect her. A disturbing encounter, but it could have been much worse.

Overdose

On another night, a call from charlie-charlie: 'Street Pastors, would you assist a very drunk woman?'

The leader recounts:

We came across a young woman who was reportedly very drunk, lapsing in and out of consciousness.

We were told she had fallen in the pub car park and that one of the pub door staff had called an ambulance.

As we stayed waiting with her, she told us that she had 'taken stuff and drunk a lot'.

I sensed that she had intense sad emotions that caused me and the team great concern.

She went on to tell us, 'I'm really concerned about my exam results, and my family don't seem to understand.'

We called the young woman's family. Her father and sister arrived about thirty minutes before the ambulance did.

The father was really concerned about his daughter, and told the team, 'I have been really worried about her for some time. We know that she has needed help, and have been trying to help, but offers of help have been refused. We don't know what to do.'

In all it took an hour and three-quarters for the ambulance to arrive. As a team we stayed with the young woman, and now the father and sister, for all of that time. When the ambulance arrived, it took the young woman to A&E. The father and sister followed by car.

It was not until the next evening, when a different Street Pastors team was out, that the doorman gave the new team some more background information: 'The young woman was really worried about her exam results, and thought she had failed one, so she took a load of sleeping pills. She then fell over and put a massive dent on her head. I went to help her, and charlie-charlie, who had been monitoring the situation, then called you guys.'

The team thanked the doorman for all he had done, which quite possibly might have assisted in saving this young woman's life.

End of the night call

Moving on from the above incidents, an outline of an entire evening, ending in a call from charlie-charlie to help someone threatening suicide:

We set out onto the streets at our usual time of around 10pm. As we wander past the clubs and pubs in the first round, we get chatting to different door staff.

'I'm from Northern Ireland, mixed Protestant and Catholic background. I've only been here about a month. I've not seen you guys before. What do you do?'

We give him a brief outline of what Street Pastors does, before moving on.

Outside another pub another doorman tells us, 'I've been in the army and served in both Iraq and Northern Ireland, but I am doing security work for now.'

We talk for a while about some of the issues we come across on the streets.

At the next pub, we meet a lively, bright and friendly group of about four or five people in their late teens or early twenties, playing a drinking game.

'We each have a card with the names of different drinks on it. We're going from pub to pub to try to get all the drinks on our list ticked off.'

We assume the winner is the one who gets the most drinks ticked off and hope they're safe and won't need our help later.

At around 11pm we come across the first homeless person of the evening.

'Would you like a sandwich?'

'Can you get me something hot, please?' We get him some chips, which he gratefully receives.

At about the same time, we see one of the regular homeless women who is probably in her fifties or so. You could almost mistake her for a bundle of clothes in a shop doorway, as she lies huddled in her sleeping bag for the night.

'Can we give you some food or water?' But she says she's OK.

Soon another regular homeless person we have seen around for a year or so appears, ex-army, wearing camouflage fatigues.

He is red-faced and shivering profusely. It's near to freezing. Although he is a bit the worse for drink, he is pleasant and friendly.

Admonishing us slightly for being out on the streets so late at night, he tells us, 'Look after yourselves and keep safe.'

We offer him a sandwich and prayer. He gratefully accepts both.

We pass a couple more pubs and have good conversations with the door staff at both venues, before heading back for our first break.

Outside one of the pubs we give out some lollies to some of the young people hanging around outside. The doorman asks, 'Can I have some, please? They'll be good for any problem clients we get later on.' We give him a handful of lollies and head back for our break.

Just before our first break, around midnight, we meet a young man from Ireland in his mid-twenties, who has been in England for several years.

'I'm really missing my girlfriend; she's in Ireland for the weekend,' he tells us, going on to say, 'I really appreciate what you guys do. I think that you guys and my girlfriend are the only ones who care.'

He's slightly drunk, and starts to open up to us about his depression, anxiety and panic attacks.

We spend about ten minutes talking to him and he tells us that at times he has thought of suicide.

We give him a Samaritans card and a Street Pastors card. Together these have several numbers he can phone to get help.

It was good to meet this young man some months later, when he thanked Street Pastors by saying, 'Thanks so much for speaking to me when you did. I'm feeling much better now.'

After our break we go out for the second round, and soon come across a young woman who has hurt her ankle.

'Would you like some flip flops?'

'No, thanks, I'm going into a club soon.'

We continue to walk around the town until about 2am, when we have our second break. It remains quiet for most of this round, with most young people in the clubs, and by now most of the homeless have probably found a spot to sleep.

Around 2.30am, the team leaves base for the final round of the evening and soon comes across two women in their twenties.

One of them says, 'I'd really like to be a Street Pastor.' We give her a card and let her know she can come out as an observer if she wants to.

Soon after this we meet a woman who appears to be alone, so we start talking to her. Her boyfriend, who was across the road getting a cab, turns up and says, 'Thanks for your concern. Are you from a local authority?' We tell him briefly what we do.

The evening stays relatively quiet. We remain outside a club for about twenty minutes or so, giving out flip flops to barefoot clubbers, before walking on and doing the same again outside another club.

It's now about 3.45am, and we are thinking of turning in, when we get a call from charlie-charlie.

'Street Pastors, can you assist a woman who has been sleeping outside a club? She's just woken up, really stressed and threatening suicide.'

We head off, on the way phoning through to the Prayer Pastors team to pray for this young woman.

In about five minutes we come across a tearful young woman in her late teens or early twenties, sitting on the streets outside a shop. A female Street Pastor sits down beside her.

'How can we help you?'

As part of a longer conversation she tells the Street Pastor, 'I've been feeling suicidal for some time.'

As a team we discuss the situation and agree that, for the woman's safety, there is no option but to call an ambulance. We relay this to charlie-charlie who have continued to monitor the situation. They call an ambulance.

We wait with this tearful and troubled young woman in the early hours of the morning, with dawn not far away.

The ambulance arrives in about ten minutes. We brief them, hoping the young woman gets the help she needs.

Concluding remarks

Such encounters can leave a person feeling emotionally drained. If need be, at the end of every evening, there is a chance to debrief with other team members and to conclude with prayer. Additional chances to debrief are also available during the following days with team coordinators and others as needed.

It is impossible to quantify how important prayer could be in such encounters. Street Pastors believes prayer is a key part of being in the right place at the right time, and as a help to give wisdom and understanding in sensitive scenarios. Additionally, the suicidal individuals in such scenarios would be the object of prayers for their safety and well-being, both on the night and for the future.

Chapter 7
Safeguarding

Safeguarding is everyone's responsibility. It is about people and organisations working together to prevent and reduce the risks and experience of abuse or neglect.

The Street Pastors movement has a national Safeguarding Policy which includes the directives that each initiative is responsible for recruiting volunteers and training, supporting and supervising them to adopt best practice to safeguard and protect children and vulnerable adults from abuse, and to minimise risk to themselves. Volunteers are required to adopt and abide by the Street Pastors Safeguarding Policy for Children and Vulnerable Adults and the procedures.

The Old Testament contains various references to God's concern for the well-being of people who are powerless and prone to being taken advantage of, in those days largely the poor, widows and orphans.

> Don't mistreat widows or orphans.[86]
> Don't take advantage of widows, orphans, visitors, and the poor.[87]

---

[86] Exodus 22:22.
[87] Zechariah 7:10.

In the New Testament, Jesus clearly showed compassion to those regarded as the least in society. People with dreaded skin complaints, disabilities and mental health issues were treated as rejects, outcasts. Women and children were not highly valued. However, using children as a visual aid, Jesus turned society's values upside down.

> Whoever becomes simple and elemental again, like this child, will rank high in God's kingdom. What's more, when you receive the childlike on my account, it's the same as receiving me.
>
> But if you give them a hard time, bullying or taking advantage of their simple trust, you'll soon wish you hadn't.[88]

In the twenty-first century, those principles influence the way our society treats those who are vulnerable to abuse and exploitation. When Street Pastors are training, all volunteers complete a Safeguarding Awareness module and learn about different types of abuse, in particular child abuse and neglect. They are taught:

> Abuse may consist of a single act or repeated acts. It may be physical, verbal or psychological, it may be an act of neglect or an omission to act, or it may occur when a vulnerable person is persuaded to enter into a financial or sexual transaction to which he or she has not consented, or cannot consent. Abuse can occur in

---

[88] Matthew 18:4-6.

any relationship and may result in significant harm to, or exploitation of the person subjected to it.[89]

In practice, Street Pastors may give special attention to children, either alone or in a group, out wandering the streets late at night, or give significant support to people who disclose or present as having been or are currently being at risk of harm.

Where Street Pastors have a safeguarding duty to a child or vulnerable adult, the top priority must always be to keep them safe but, where possible, they will also try to respect the rights, wishes, feelings and beliefs of individuals involved when making a decision. Immense wisdom, tact and discretion are needed.

The following reports from two different patrol nights in the Greater London area illustrate how the teams addressed complex safeguarding issues while maintaining respect for the human rights and dignity of the people concerned. The incidents described demonstrate good practice where Street Pastors liaised with statutory and other appropriate agencies and abided by non-discriminatory principles. In the first case, a team was confronted by both financial and sexual abuse issues.

A woman at risk

Around 10.30pm, outside a local pub we saw a rough sleeper, a woman, approach a group of customers and

---

[89] 'No Secrets: guidance on protecting vulnerable adults in care', https://www.gov.uk/government/publications/no-secrets-guidance-on-protecting-vulnerable-adults-in-care (accessed 4th July 2020).

beg from them. They gave her £20, which she immediately passed to her male companion, saying, 'There. Why do you complain about me? I've got £20 for you, haven't I?'

When we spoke to the woman, she told us she was called Kath, and asked for a sleeping bag. She agreed to meet us outside a local shop in half an hour. Kath said she'd been homeless for nine months, and looked about thirty years old.

Her companion, who called himself Mike and was probably ten years older, said he was homeless but lodging with a friend.

'I'm staying with Kath to protect her and look after her,' Mike said, before adding, 'I think she's selling herself on the streets. I don't like to think she is having sex with other men. We've been on and off partners for the last nine months.'

Two of the team talked to him about his struggles to give up alcohol and how difficult it was to keep occupied. They offered some suggestions, but they were not well received.

We all agreed to meet up with them both later, so we could give Kath a sleeping bag. Mike said, 'I think she's pregnant, but I'm not sure 'cos she isn't always honest with me.'

After a while we left and made our way back to base to pick up a sleeping bag for Kath. Shortly afterwards we found them again outside the main shopping centre and handed over the sleeping bag.

'Thanks so much,' she said, giving us each a big hug.

Returning to base for a quick cup of tea, we had a call from the people manning the town's CCTV system: 'Street Pastors, please can you assist with a woman who is self-harming?' They gave us the name of the club and a contact name.

We quickly downed our drinks and headed for the club, where the doorman said he was concerned about a young woman who was self-harming and had a cut on her wrist which was bleeding. He said she was with a man, tall and bearded, in his forties wearing a duffel coat. It sounded very much like Kath and Mike, so we doubled back in search of Kath.

On our way we encountered two women, both rough sleepers and rather drunk. The older woman said she wanted to go to hospital, that she suffered with significant health issues. As we were debating whether to call her an ambulance, two police officers came over who recognised the older woman. They advised us to call the non-emergency number 101, which we did, and they said that they would send an ambulance. The younger woman admitted she now lived in a house share thanks to a charity and was due to begin a three-week residential detox programme.

While waiting for the ambulance we spoke to another rough sleeper, who told us that he too was concerned about Kath. He had seen her bleeding from the wrist and that she had got into a car, which he described. He had even memorised the first part of the registration number. Then he told us he thought Mike was pimping her.

As soon as the ambulance arrived, we made straight to the police station to report what the rough sleeper had told us about Kath.

It was more than an hour since we had received the call, and we had still not found Kath, which was worrying. We met some rough sleepers bedded down outside a big department store. There was evidence of heroin use, the telltale signs of a belt and teaspoons lying about.

'Is Kath with you?' we called out.

'No,' came back the reply.

Finally, just after 3am we found Kath outside a pizza restaurant. She walked straight up to us.

'You told the police on me.'

'What happened?'

'The police found me and questioned me.'

'What happened when you got into the car?'

'I had sex. Made 50 quid.'

'Did anyone make you do it?' our team leader asked.

'No.'

'Is there anything we can do to help you feel safe?'

'I'm just getting money together for alcohol for me and my friends. I can take care of myself, but thanks.'

'What are you going to do now?'

'I'm going to meet Mike. He's got my sleeping bag.'

It was a relief to have met her, though we were still concerned about her vulnerability.

Shortly afterwards we met and spoke with two policemen about Kath. They turned out to be the same policemen who had questioned Kath earlier.

'She gave us her full name, her age and showed us the cuts on her wrist. We considered they were non-life-threatening so we couldn't section her,' they told us.

'Did she tell you that she had had sex for £50 tonight?'

'No, she didn't. You need to report that to the front office at the police station.'

We duly arrived at the front office and reported what we knew. We added that Kath was going to sleep outside with Mike. We also recounted the incident at the beginning of the evening when she begged for money and gave it to Mike. We returned to base where we prayed for Kath and the others. We had done our best to keep her safe.

Following due protocol, a safeguarding report for Kath and for her suspected unborn child was completed and sent to the appropriate council department.

Teenager

The following case from the same area shows how a potentially vulnerable teenage woman was helped by the combined efforts of Street Pastors, the relevant statutory bodies and an alert member of the public:

Towards midnight we were walking down the main pedestrianised high street when we were flagged down by a man in his early thirties who was sitting on a bench which he was sharing with a young woman.

'I found this girl sitting here alone. She's called Lily and she's fifteen years old,' he told us.

Lily seemed very frightened but was very reluctant to talk to us. Another man approached us to say he had just returned from a night shelter where he had gone to tell them about this young woman, hoping they could persuade her to go and sit in the shelter, so she wasn't sitting out in the cold on her own.

Lily refused point blank to go to the shelter, emphatically denied that she was called Lily and would not tell us where she lived. After a lot of gentle cajoling we managed to find out the name of her home town and that a reputable care agency was involved in her welfare. She clearly trusted the agency and had confidence in them. Unfortunately, as hard as we tried, we were unable to find an out-of-hours number for that agency.

We told her we couldn't find the number and she replied, 'It's OK. I live with my mum and brother.'

'We'll phone your mum for you,' we offered.

'I don't want you to phone them. Anyway, I haven't got my phone and I don't want you to do anything.'

With safeguarding uppermost in our minds, we felt that we couldn't just leave her sitting on the bench.

'I'm staying here. I'm waiting for someone to collect me,' she said.

Thankfully, after some gentle probing she told us she had a named social worker whom she was expecting to arrive soon.

While we were talking, a police car drove up and stopped. Lily was clearly very unhappy about this new development. She had already told us in no uncertain terms that she didn't want the police involved, which would have been our next step.

However, what we didn't know was that the first man who had alerted us to Lily had phoned the national call centre, Childline, and given them details about her. Childline had managed to identify and call her social worker, who in turn had phoned the police.

When the police explained they had been called by her social worker, whom they named, Lily visibly relaxed. They offered to take Lily back to the police station where she could phone her social worker. So Lily willingly accompanied the police to the station.

We were so relieved and very grateful for the quick response of the police, the care and sensitivity with which they spoke to her and the thoughtfulness of the member of public. Under the circumstances, it was the best possible outcome. When we returned to base, we thanked the Prayer Pastors who had been praying throughout.

Chapter 8
Street Pastors in the North-East

Chris Lincoln moved to Newcastle in the 1980s with his work, and as such knows the area well. He retired in 2002, and for the last eleven years, since 2009, has volunteered as a Street Pastor – in Newcastle upon Tyne for two years, and then for about eight years in Whitley Bay, where he is the team coordinator. He also set up Jesmond Street Pastors in 2016 and is the team coordinator for this group, as well as for Whitley Bay.

In addition to his work with Street Pastors, Chris has done considerable work with the homeless. For the past five winters, this has included leading the operational side of Severe Weather Emergency Protocol (SWEP). SWEP is an initiative of North Tyneside Council to take the rough sleepers off the streets when temperatures drop to 'real feel' minus degrees during the winter months November to March. 'Real feel' temperatures account for extra chill factors, such as wind, that can make it feel much colder than the recorded temperature.

To run SWEP, Chris manages a team of forty-five volunteers, which includes some Street Pastors, some Prayer Pastors, some church members and others.

The teams look after the guests from 7pm to 8am, providing them with a hot meal and a warm bed for the night, using their base at a church as accommodation. They also work with the council to try to get accommodation for their guests.

Chris says, 'As a new Christian in 2008, I felt I wanted to make a difference outside of the church, by caring for the vulnerable.'

Here Chris writes about the areas in which he has volunteered as a Street Pastor, about his training, some of his experiences and some of the local Street Pastors initiatives he has been involved in.

The Toon

In the fifties and sixties in the Toon (a nickname for Newcastle upon Tyne based on the local dialect pronunciation), for those working down the pit (local coal mine), the shipyard and other heavy industries, drinking was the main social relaxation. Nightclubs sprang up in many towns and working men's clubs were found in most villages.

In the nineties and today, Newcastle's boisterous pubs, bars and clubs are concentrated in several areas. These include the Bigg Market, around the Quayside, in the developing Ouseburn area, where bars tend to be quirkier and more sophisticated; in Jesmond, with its thriving student-filled strip of cafés and bars; and in the mainstream leisure and cinema complex, known as The Gate. There are also a lot of bars in an area known as the Pink Triangle, between the Central Station and the Metro Radio Arena.

Visitors are encouraged to think of the city as Newcastle–Gateshead, an amalgamation of both Newcastle upon Tyne and Gateshead, both straddling the Tyne.

On Gateshead Quays one can find the Baltic Centre for Contemporary Art and the Sage music centre. On the opposite side of the river, Newcastle's Quayside is a scene of much of the city's contemporary nightlife.

The city splits into several distinct areas, though it's only a matter of minutes to walk between them. The castle and cathedral occupy the heights immediately above the River Tyne. North of these is the city centre, also known as Grainger Town, the historic heart of the city, with many of the city's finest buildings and streets. Chinatown, the Discovery Museum and the Life Science Centre are west of the centre; east of the city centre is the renowned Laing Art Gallery.

In the north of the city, on the university campus, is the Great North Museum: Hancock. Further north, through the landscaped Exhibition Park, is the Town Moor, 1,200 acres of common land where freemen of the city – including Jimmy Carter, Bob Geldof and the late Nelson Mandela – are entitled to graze their cattle.

Added to all this are the large universities, which bring more than 50,000 students to the Toon from all over the world. Pubs and clubs offer special student nights and cheap drinks offers.

Stag weekends and hen nights can add to the already busyness of the Toon. In 2009, when I was doing my Street Pastors training, I remember hearing that most weekends alone, 60,000 people visited the city centre.

Training and first night out

Street Pastors was launched in the Toon in 2008. My wife and I joined in August 2009. Having gone through the interview and having had references completed, we started the training.

In the past, I used to be out in the Toon on a Saturday night, and I knew most of the venues. I'd even fallen out of some. I felt apprehensive about meeting some of the people I had known from the past, but I had a reassurance that God would be walking with us on patrol.

As the weeks of training went by, friendships started and these continued later on when we began to go out on patrol. Each of us had different skills and strengths to contribute. The medical members of the team were very popular.

I remember the first aid training, which was just good fun, singing along to 'Nellie the Elephant' as we practised CPR. Now it's 'Staying Alive', quite an apt song given what is being learnt.

Our first aid training also included how to deal with asthmatic episodes, head injuries, foot injuries, hypothermia and more. There was so much for us to remember as we prepared for our first night on the streets.

Following our commissioning, which was part of a wonderful church service, we were ready to go out onto the streets for the first time.

Our meeting place for patrols was a room in the cathedral, an imposing building in the Toon. This was ideal, as it was so central.

That first night of patrol, as I parked my car, I recall hearing all the noises of the Toon at night. The traffic, the sirens, the shouting and screaming, and a sound that would become all too familiar: the sound of a glass bottle breaking as it hit the ground.

That first night there were several other new recruits who were on their first patrol. We checked the Street Pastors rucksack for water, flip flops, tissues, wipes, chocolate and the first aid kit.

Looking around the room as I put on my winter jacket, I noticed there were anxious looks from those on their first night. Would we remember what our training had taught us, what to say when asked, 'What's a Street Pastor?'

The team leader led us in prayer. There were two teams that night. I was in a team that would head up the Bigg Market to The Gate complex, a very busy part of the Toon. My wife was on the other team.

Bags packed and hats on, we headed out, to be met by the smell of pizzas, kebabs, chips, aftershave and vomit.

Waiting to cross the road, two lads thanked us for what we do. 'You are amazing. Keep safe; we might see you later,' they said, before running across the road on a red light, as taxis screeched to a halt and drivers shook their fists. They disappeared into the crowds, laughing.

As we walked up the Bigg Market, our team leader spoke to the door staff. A mass of yellow-jacketed police officers waved as we walked by. Police seemed to be everywhere that night.

Moments later, our leader stopped to listen to and speak into her radio, which was connected to camera control. 'We've just been called to The Gate complex. The police have found a very drunk female,' she told us.

When we arrived, the female was on the ground, where the police had found her. They weren't sure if she was with friends and asked us, 'Can we leave her with you? We need to deal with a fight in the next street.'

As the police left us, four more women arrived. They were her friends, but weren't keen to be around with the police. They weren't too happy with their friend, telling us, 'She was determined to get bladdered' (a new word I learned that night, meaning to get very drunk). Her friends quickly decided that we were going to look after her. They wanted to go back to the pub, where they had met four Scottish lads on a stag weekend.

Our leader disagreed with their strategy and told them, 'You need to get your friend home before continuing your night out.'

After what seemed like ages, one of the women rang her brother, who agreed to come into town, for a price, to take this woman home.

In the meantime, we had put a space blanket around the woman to keep her warm, and supplied her with water.

The brother arrived. The woman we were looking after had sobered up a bit by that time. As she knew the brother, she was content to get a lift home with him. Her friends quickly disappeared into the pub, only to return moments later to shout at us that the boys had gone.

Before we left, we thanked God in prayer that her friends were nearby and had arranged a lift home for her.

These types of situations we see on a regular basis. In general, we follow a similar process, if possible, getting friends to help us get the vulnerable person home.

As we moved on, some security guards ran past us and shouted that they needed our help.

On the ground was a woman having a seizure. We used one of our coats to try to protect her head. She was thrashing about. An ambulance had been called and it eventually arrived, much to our relief. The ambulance crew appeared to know her and picked her up and took her to the ambulance.

The security staff thanked us, and asked, 'Can we offer you a tea, coffee or juice?'

'No, thanks, probably see you later, though, stay safe.' We picked our things up and dispensed with our disposable gloves, before moving on.

As we walked through The Gate, I was amazed at the number of people who stopped us to thank us for what we do. For some reason, many of those who stopped asked for pasta – carbonara, I think, was the most popular request – or a pasty. Fortunately, we could direct them to a local takeaway. Written on the back of our jackets are the words 'Street Pastor'. I think with a little too much alcohol the 'Pastor' had in their eyes become 'Pasta' or 'Pasty'!

We had time then to go in for a short break and complete our report cards. These allow us to record the events of the night and help us give details of the service we provide for the community.

I have learned over the years to put the kettle on before we leave the base. This is because we often get called to help someone during our breaks, so we need to get the kettle boiled quickly. Especially in winter, when the northerly wind is howling, it's not unusual to have negative temperatures. It's vital the team get a warm drink into them and a snack, to keep up energy levels.

At the end of the night, after helping with other situations, it was good to catch up with my wife, Jackie, and hear her stories. Jackie, being a member of the NHS, had been involved in some more-serious situations. Her previous experiences in the NHS had been invaluable. When we got home at 4am we put the kettle on. We spent another two to three hours excitedly recapping our first patrol.

I feel very blessed that Jackie is also a Street Pastor, which means we can share so much of this wonderful journey together.

Football

Football plays a huge part in the life of the Geordies.[90] Home games usually attract about 50,000 fans and they usually sell all their away tickets. If the match is on a Saturday at home and they win, after the match, many stay behind, mingling with the happy-hour drinkers, so the party starts early; usually those bars with the best offers are full by teatime, and drinkers move from pub to pub. So by the time we arrive on the streets, we meet lots of people who are struggling from drinking excess alcohol.

---

[90] A person from Tyneside.

We have to be ready from the moment the team leader signs in to the control centre, as calls come in very quickly. One night when Jackie did her radio sign-in, the person at the control centre responded by saying, 'Are you sure you want to come out tonight? It's really busy.' Just one of many lively nights we experience.

Hen and stag nights

The Toon is popular for hen and stag nights. People come from all over the country, staying in one of the many hotels. A party of twenty to thirty people is not unusual, all dressed in their themed costumes, some with signs indicating Mother of Hen, Bridesmaid, Aunt, Grandma and, of course, Bride.

On one of the patrols, we came across a very distressed female sitting on the ground outside the central railway station. She was using her phone, and once she had finished her call, a female member of the team went over and sat with her, to talk to her and understand how we might help. It transpired that she was on a hen night with friends from Carlisle. Unfortunately, the minibus had gone, her friends had left her, and there were no trains to Carlisle until early morning.

She had been speaking to her mother on the phone, so we rang her mother back to say she was with us and safe. Her parents agreed to collect her and were on their way from Carlisle, so we took her back to our base to wait for them to arrive. Carlisle is about ninety minutes away, on a good journey. She was safe, though, and her parents didn't have worry or speed across to get her.

Bank holidays and a missing pet

Bank holiday weekends are even busier. One such bank holiday we had a different call for assistance – a woman on a mobility scooter was in a distressed state and needed help.

As we headed to where she was, we started to discuss what the call may be for; perhaps she had broken down. Could you call the RAC for a broken-down mobility scooter?

On our journey, we saw two men who looked as if they had just come off a building site, with what looked like a small dog. In the distance we could see the woman on her mobility scooter. When we arrived, we spoke to the door staff who had called us. They told us, 'She's lost her pet hairless chihuahua.'

So what we had seen with the two men – could that be the chihuahua? We made a call to camera control: 'Please can someone apprehend two men with a stolen chihuahua!'

Ten minutes later, we received a response from some bar staff via camera control: 'We have the two men and the chihuahua.'

We told the woman, who was overjoyed. We started the slow journey with her to the bar to pick up her chihuahua. On the way, she told us it was called Mad Max, that it always came out with her and sat in the fur-lined basket at the front of the scooter.

When we reached the bar there was a wonderful reunion. She thanked us, turned her scooter around and headed back into the night.

Whitley Bay

Twenty-four months into my Street Pastors journey, I left Newcastle Street Pastors team to become coordinator of the newly established Whitley Bay Street Pastors team, in 2011. I had learned so much and wanted to set my new team up in the same manner as the team I was leaving.

Whitley Bay, a small coastal town joined to Cullercoats and Tynemouth, had its own popular night life. Not on the scale of Newcastle, but nevertheless very popular with the locals.

We established ourselves as valuable responders in the community. A mobile safe place was provided for us by the local authority, and we set off on weekly patrols in Whitley Bay and Tynemouth.

When I first moved to Whitley Bay, I felt blessed that a Prayer Pastors team was also in the process of being set up. During the eight years we have been operational, this group has prayed faithfully every night we have been out on patrol, which has been a great support to us.

Since Whitley Bay Street Pastors has been running, we have been invited to do Metro patrols, bike patrols along the seafront, to have a presence at the Mouth of the Tyne Festival and to do talks in schools.

The Metro is a transport system similar to London's Underground, in and around Newcastle. Weekends on the Metro can be troublesome, with the young ones causing significant problems. We were invited to participate in Metro patrols on a Friday night, as part of a joint police operation. So, on Friday nights, a team of three Street Pastors sat on the Metro, in uniform, riding from Wallsend to Northumberland Park and back again, just having a presence. This calmed the young ones down and the older passengers gave us great feedback. When the police operation finished, we continued on our own for another year.

The Mouth of the Tyne Festival is a four-day annual festival, held in July and organised by North Tyneside Council. It is held in the grounds of the priory at Tynemouth, which is an amazing venue. We are asked to support the event, with our vehicle, looking after the vulnerable ones who have drunk too much. It can be busy. The people attending the event can take in as much alcohol as they wish.

When we first set up in Whitley Bay, we attended secondary schools' morning assemblies, to explain what we did in the night-time economy. We now attend the secondary schools regularly as Street Pastors is part of the Religious Studies curriculum.

Response Pastors

I trained to be a Response Pastor in 2016 in Sheffield. Five of us from my Street Pastors team travelled down together for the training, meeting up with others from Yorkshire teams.

On the night of Monday 22nd May 2017, I was watching TV at home when the news broke of the Manchester Arena bombing, when 23 people, including the perpetrator, were killed in a terrorist attack at a pop concert. The next day a message came from Ascension Trust, asking for volunteers. I volunteered for the Friday. I travelled down by train and was asked to lead a small team of three or four people from different parts of the country. One of the team had been deployed the previous day, so she was able to hand down the briefing regarding the deployment area.

Arriving in St Ann's Square, what struck me was the quietness in the heart of the city. At the top end of the square there was a bank of TV cameras, but below them a vast sea of the most colourful flowers I had ever seen. People were laying flowers, businesses were arriving with huge displays and then, later in the day, chalk messages were left on the pavement.

Armed police were everywhere, watching, listening, eyes peeled on the vast crowds of people. The sound of sirens had everyone looking nervous. An armed policeman came across and asked us if we could help a diabetic who was feeling unwell as he hadn't eaten. We quickly moved to help him, gave him a biscuit and stayed with him until he had recovered.

It was packed that day; lots of elderly people were in town for the first time since the bombing. They reminded us of the IRA attack some twenty years earlier, in June 1996. People hadn't dared to come into town until now as they thought there could be another bomb, as was rumoured after the bomb in the 1996 IRA attack.

Wearing a Response Pastor tabard, we were asked, 'Are you like those Street Pastors?' We explained that we *were* Street Pastors.

One man commented, 'You aren't from around here, are you?'

'No, I'm from Newcastle.'

He couldn't believe all of the team had travelled to Manchester to stand with the locals at their time of need.

I remember that day we prayed with so many people: those who knew someone who had been to the concert; for Manchester to rebuild as it had after the IRA attack; for those injured in hospital; for the families of those who had lost a loved one. There were many handshakes and hugs that day as we stood with the Manchester people in their hour of need.

The day finished with prayer, reflecting on the many we had stood with. I reminded the team that if they wished to talk through their day, a help and support line had been set up by Ascension Trust.

I think we deployed teams on the Tuesday, Wednesday, Thursday, Friday, Saturday and Sunday after the Arena attack.

We finished around 7pm so we could get our trains home. As I sat on the train reflecting on the day, little did I know that two weeks later I would be heading to London for three days after the Borough Market terrorist attack.[91]

In conclusion

To conclude, Chris says, 'I feel blessed to be able to volunteer in my community and to be God's hands, His eyes and His feet on the streets, caring for the vulnerable.'

---

[91] You can read about this incident in Chapter 10.

Chapter 9
Stories from Northern Ireland

From 1968 to 1998, this small, beautiful region suffered three decades of violence and hostility, with its population divided by religious beliefs, economics and politics. The turmoil became known as 'The Troubles' and resulted in the loss of some 3,000 people, with many more adversely affected by bereavement, physical injury or trauma.

In a 2011 census, 83 per cent of the population described themselves as Christian (compared to 59 per cent in England). In this census people identified as Catholic, 41 per cent; Protestant or other, 42 per cent; no religion, 17 per cent and other religions and philosophies, less than 1 per cent.[92]

During The Troubles, although many perceived themselves as Christians, the country was riven by violence and hostility between religious groups. Yet at the same time, churches of all persuasions mobilised themselves to actively work for and plead for peace and reconciliation. Individuals, charities and movements

---

[92] Northern Ireland statistics and research centre, www.ninis2.nisra.gov.uk/public (accessed 4th July 2020).

emerged to bring healing, hope and reconciliation between very disparate groups.

Street Pastors, being an interdenominational organisation, is ideally placed to help in this crucial healing process. There are five Street Pastors initiatives, in Ards and North Down; Belfast; Coleraine and Ballymoney; Newtonabbey; Lisburn and Castlereagh. We are going to look more closely at the Coleraine branch and its work in Portrush, a small seaside town.

The Coleraine branch was established in October 2014, its volunteers coming from thirty local Christian churches of varying denominations and helping to strengthen Church unity in the area. It patrols every weekend, and in common with all Street Pastors initiatives, it works in partnership with the police, local council and other statutory agencies.

On Friday nights the team patrols different areas of Coleraine and on Saturday nights it patrols the small ports of Portstewart and Portrush, listening, caring and helping.

Portrush has a population of 6,442[93] and is home to the largest nightclub in the whole of Northern Ireland, which attracts many famous DJs and hosts BBC Radio 1 events. In nearby Coleraine is the campus of the Ulster University, and at weekends many students enjoy visiting this nightclub in Portrush.

The religious demographics of Portrush are similar to the population of Northern Ireland as a whole. On Census Day in 2011, residents of Portrush considered

---

[93] City population, 'Portrush 2011', www.citypopulation.de/php/uk-northernireland.php?cityid=N11000183 (accessed 4th July 2020).

themselves as 83.9 per cent Christian and 15.3 per cent no religion.

Here, Wilhelmina, a long-standing member of Coleraine Street Pastors, shares some stories from her personal experience of patrolling Portrush.

From the Diary of a Street Pastor, aged seventy-eight

My first Saturday night out

From my very first night out in Portrush, when I was rather nervous and a little apprehensive, I will never forget the quite unexpected sense of compassion I experienced. It was overwhelming.

As I observed the young people pouring out of a large nightclub, having expected to be quite critical of them 'wasting their own parents' money', I saw them as my own grandchildren – any sense of criticism simply disappeared.

New Year's Eve

It was a bitterly cold night and the busiest night I have ever experienced. We started out at 10pm and finished at 4am. There was lots to do, many people to help and many conversations, which distracted me from the excessive cold. I was wearing four layers on both my top and bottom half – how the young people survive wearing skimpy dance-wear beats me.

We started off well with New Year greetings and friendly banter. We received many expressions of gratitude, 'Fair play to ya!' and such like. A Royal Navy guy thanked us profusely as he had been in Sydney at that time the previous year where he had been very much the worse for drink. 'Street Pastors like you helped me. I mightn't be alive today if they hadn't been there,' he admitted.

Another young man also thanked us repeatedly. One night he'd received a cut on his upper lip and the Street Pastors had applied first aid and got him to A&E. He proudly showed us the scar.

My first intervention came ten minutes after midnight with a young couple fighting in front of an ATM. I asked if I could help. The man had wanted to kiss his partner on the stroke of midnight and was 'raging mad' that she wouldn't allow him. We managed to calm them both down and they went off in a lighter mood, though they had still not had that longed-for embrace.

We encountered many angry young women. The first was a young blonde woman who had to be taken away in a police van, having broken a police officer's little finger. Then we came across a woman who looked unconscious. A caring young man was supporting by letting her sit on his knees, but she was utterly unresponsive. I managed to extricate her phone from her tight grip. We prayed silently as the young man tried to access her mum's phone number and, thankfully, he succeeded. We called her parents, who were only a short distance away in their car on the promenade. Within minutes, an older man appeared, claiming to be her father (he showed us some ID to confirm his identity). He tried to lift her, but she was a dead weight, so we asked him to bring the car nearer, which he did. The poor mother was so distressed when she saw her daughter.

'I have *never* seen her like this – and she has to fly back to England tomorrow,' she exclaimed.

We had to cover her daughter with two space blankets to protect her modesty and it needed all four of us to lift her down the few steps into her parents' car, her feet dragging along the ground. She was still not responding in any way.

Following this we met another aggressive, dark-haired woman, swearing profusely, who, on being evicted from a bar, had removed her shoes and hurled them at the door staff. They happily confiscated them. We gave her a pair of flip flops and kept an eye on her as she walked off in her 'new' shoes.

We came across a young man abandoned by his friends. He was so drunk and ashen white and so sick that no taxi was prepared to take him. We wrapped him in a space blanket and left him in a sheltered area at about 3.20am. We reported this to the police, who called us later when we returned to base. They were checking that he was not injured or unconscious. The police were under tremendous pressure that evening and could only deal with more-serious cases.

We received a delightful comment from two women: 'I can see the love in your eyes, even behind your specs,' which was so encouraging.

St Patrick's Day
Around 9pm on another really cold night we walked around to two of the big bars, but we were far too early

for the night-time revellers. There were lots of them going to and fro between the two bars, but it was difficult to 'connect'. A Christian youth club was running an alternative event in the Town Hall, so we dropped in to chat with them – not very successfully, as the music was deafening.

Our first main intervention was with an angry young woman who had been evicted from a bar for being extremely drunk. One of the door staff had lifted her physically and dumped her at the corner by a church.

A male team member and I approached her, but she reversed away from us, screaming, 'Go away! Go away!' We hovered around, just in case she might change her mind. Shortly afterwards, the police arrived. We were most impressed with the way the policeman and policewoman handled her. They were really kind and caring, coaxing and persuading, eventually getting her into the patrol car and taking her home.

Outside a pub, a most garrulous middle-aged man wanted to engage us in 'theological conversation'. He was from Derry and had some seriously strange ideas about Jesus, God, Buddha and so on, a right mishmash of beliefs. I encouraged him to try to come to an Alpha course group held on Monday nights in a pub, where he could indulge his interest in theological discussion.[94]

---

[94] The Alpha course runs over eleven weeks and provides an opportunity for people to find out more about the Christian faith and what it means to be a Christian. On each night participants are served a three-course meal, hear a thought-provoking talk and join in with informal discussions. See alpha.org (accessed 30th June 2020).

It was quite an odd evening, as normally people come up to us and chat, but tonight there was quite a different crowd. It was a bitterly cold night, with a strong, driving wind funnelling up from the promenade, so it was no surprise that the women wanted to get inside the bars as soon as possible.

About a quarter to midnight, just as our leader suggested we should head back to base, suddenly everything livened up. A lovely young woman came over, still clutching her wine bottle, and was most keen to talk. She insisted on having a whip-round among her friends to give us a donation.

'You people do such an amazing job. All volunteers doing this for us,' she exclaimed.

Sheltered from the biting wind, we ended up having a fantastic conversation with her and three friends. One of them was telling us all how his values had changed since his mum's cancer diagnosis.

At that point I called over our observer for the night, a man who has won significant medals in self-defence. He was able to really connect with this guy and was so wise in the way he talked with him. It was a wonderful example of the value of teamwork. Then the man's business partner arrived, an estate agent who wanted to join in 'the craic'. She was a single mum from a devout Catholic family and we had a long chat with her.

Meanwhile, my male colleague was nearby in deep conversation with a young woman who resisted all encouragements by her friends to go back into the club because she simply wanted to know more about God. How cool is that?

We met a group of young teens on the corner who made some smart comment to me about doing a back flip. Along came our observer from behind me and promptly did one. He then showed them some smart self-defence moves. The boys were goggle-eyed.

We reached base at about 12.40am, for hot drinks and thankful prayers. I was home in bed by 1.20am and truly grateful for my electric blanket and a hot-water bottle.

More encounters of the remarkable kind

One wet and gloomy Friday night we had an early urgent phone call from a local Christian youth club. That night it was absolutely pelting down with rain and our Street Pastors teams were soaked through. Some teenagers from a local park where we know there is a lot of illegal drug activity ran into this Christian youth group to escape the rain. One of the teenagers sought out one of the Street Pastors, who they recognised, and shared that the real reason why they had been unable to attend school was because a close relative had taken their own life.

On another occasion we saw a young man all alone and walked towards him.

'Ha! Street Pastors! Don't talk to me about religion!' he mocked.

'No, we weren't going to, but now that you mention it, why don't you want to talk about it?' asked Ellie, another mature member of the team.

Out tumbled a story of anger against God, deep hurt because God had 'taken his father away' when he was only twenty and reasons why he would never forgive God.

'But,' he added, 'you're Street Pastors, what would you know about it?'

'Well, actually,' said Ellie, very gently, 'I would very much understand. My dad was taken from me when I was ten years old. He was killed by a drunk driver and my mother was disabled for the rest of her life.'

This opened up an amazing opportunity to reach out to this hurting young man. Ellie was able to share that she hadn't been a Christian then, but since having Jesus in her life, she had been able to forgive the drunk driver.

Some happy endings

One of the 'hard men' in a gang was giving me some lip. I laughed – but then one of the other 'hard men' commented, 'Don't mess with this woman. She prayed for me a couple of weeks ago to get a job and I'm starting work on Monday.' (It actually wasn't me but another Street Pastor granny.)

Around 2.30am my team saw a young man looking very depressed, sitting alone on a shop windowsill. He hadn't wanted to come out that night, but friends had persuaded him; now they'd all abandoned him, and he was alone with no way of getting home. One of the men from the Street Pastors team sat down beside him, realised he knew him from schooldays, and began chatting. The team sent a prayer request back to the Prayer Pastors at base. Soon after we were able to hail a taxi and see him off safely. He really brightened up, saying, 'Thank you so much. You've made my night.'

On another occasion, a woman rushed up to the Street Pastors team in a state of near desperation. 'Oh, you're Street Pastors! *Please* can you tell me how I can find God?' She described how a couple of weeks earlier she had been in a Portstewart shop, in real agony with a long-standing backache. There were no other customers in the store, so the shop owner, a Christian woman, noticing her pain, asked her if it would be OK to pray for her. She agreed – and the agonising pain disappeared. Ever since she had been searching for someone to explain to her who this amazing God was. One of the Street Pastors 'happened' to be wearing a multicoloured beaded bracelet from his church summer holiday club which he used as a visual aid to explain to her more about God.

One morning at 3.30am we had an urgent call from a Street Pastor to pray for taxis. Within five minutes we took another call from him, telling us, 'Stop praying for taxis! We have too many.'

Another night, a team member called in from an infamous nightclub. It was 3.30am and everyone apparently had gone home. Two people needed a taxi for Belfast and there was no sign of any taxis and no response to his phone calls. He'd tried several numbers. We prayed. In desperation he called one of the taxi firms back and they told him a cancellation had *just* occurred, but it was a people carrier and would have to return from Ballycastle. By the time it arrived, six more people had emerged from nowhere – needing lifts to Ballymoney, Ballymena, etc, all en route to Belfast. They all left together in the same taxi.

A concluding reflection

It would not be the whole story if as Christians we did not acknowledge that sometimes not everything has a happy ending. There are disappointments, mistakes and tragedies. Sometimes people refuse help; sometimes the same individual keeps on behaving in a self-destructive way; sometimes Street Pastors schemes struggle with raising finance or sustaining volunteer numbers.

The Bible does not airbrush out the hard facts of life – the sorrows, failings, difficulties. In the Old Testament there are stories of fallible human beings such as Abraham, Jacob, Joseph and David. In the New Testament we read about tragedies, such as new convert Stephen being stoned to death, Paul and Barnabas falling out and going their separate ways, the disciples misunderstanding Jesus. The Bible does not gloss over times when difficult and tragic things happen.

The apostle Paul, who himself experienced disappointments, beatings and imprisonment, wrote, 'Throw yourselves into the work of the Master, confident that nothing you do for him is a waste of time or effort.'[95]

Street Pastors may not always see happy endings, but they know it is vital to persevere, to follow the example

---

[95] 1 Corinthians 15:58.

of Jesus, to keep on doing good, serving any in need, even if there are troubles of one kind or another.

Chapter 10
Response, Rail and School Pastors

The problem of suffering and pain has troubled people since the beginning of time. For Christians the problem is critical, as they are often asked, 'How can you believe in a God who allows so much suffering?' It's an issue that many have tried to address, including C S Lewis, Dietrich Bonhoeffer and, in recent times, American author Philip Yancey who wrote the book *Where Is God When It Hurts?* in 1997.[96]

During a book-signing session not long after the 9/11 tragedy in New York, a man came up to him and apologised that as he had no time to read the book, could Yancey answer the question in the book title in one or two sentences. Yancey replied with another question, 'Where is the *church* when it hurts?' He then explained that if the Church was seen to be 'binding wounds, comforting the grieving, offering food to the hungry',

---

[96] Phillip Yancey, *Where Is God When It Hurts?* (Grand Rapids, MI: Zondervan, 1997, revised edition).

then people will 'know where God is: in the presence of his people on earth'.[97]

Response, Rail and School Pastors work in places where people are hurting, where there has been a major incident, at railway stations where there have been fatalities and in schools and colleges where young people need someone to confide in.

Response Pastors

Response Pastors are experienced Street Pastors who receive additional focused training so they can respond to crisis-level events less than twenty-four hours later.

They have been present in the aftermath of the Shoreham Air Crash (2015), the Croydon Tram Crash (2016), the terrorist attack on Westminster (2017), the Jo Cox Memorial (2017), the Manchester Arena bombing (2017), the London Bridge terrorist attack (2017), Finsbury Park Mosque attack (2017), the Grenfell Tower fire (2017) and the Streatham High Street terrorist attack (2020).

Response Pastors evolved after discussions between Ascension Trust, the umbrella organisation of Street Pastors, the Metropolitan Police and several regional police services, as well as local authorities' resilience forums and others involved in the operational side of major incidents and crisis situations.

The Response Pastors initiative was launched in August 2014, initially in London boroughs, and is now

---

[97] Phillip Yancey, 'Reflections on 9/11',
https://philipyancey.com/features/reflections-on-911 (accessed 4th July 2020).

established in many areas around the UK, with 150 volunteers trained in the first eighteen months of its existence.

Response Pastors can be called upon any day or night to act as a crucial point of contact and a welcome additional support to the established emergency services.

The Response Pastors national coordinator at Ascension Trust oversees this work. After hearing from a group called the London Resilience Forum, the coordinator sends out an appeal for volunteers. It is the responsibility of the forum's chairperson to receive immediate briefings from the police and in turn to contact Ascension Trust to request support. The national coordinator then needs to gauge availability of volunteers and make a risk assessment about the safety of sending volunteers to a major incident. In some cases, the national coordinator might contact the authorities directly.

The primary task of Response Pastors is to offer support and compassion to all in the event of a crisis or an emergency. This may be outside emergency cordons at an incident such as Grenfell Tower or specifically to assist in a reception centre for survivors, evacuees or other persons affected by an event.

London Bridge

On 3rd June 2017 three men were responsible for the death of eight people and injuries to forty-eight, all ordinary members of the public. The attackers, extremists inspired by Islamic State, were shot dead by Metropolitan Police officers.[98]

One member of this Response Pastors team was Chris Lincoln, who trained as a Street Pastor in 2009, then as a Response Pastor in 2016.[99] Chris was deployed for three days as a Response Pastor.

Arriving on the Tuesday afternoon, I headed for St Magnus the Martyr church, our base to meet up with the team. After a few quick hellos and a briefing from the woman leading the day, we prayed. I sensed a wonderful togetherness among the teams. Then we headed out, crossing London Bridge.

The entrance to Borough High Street was closed. This was where the van had crashed before the terrorists started to attack. As we were in uniform, the press recognised us. They stayed close by as we talked with those paying their respects by laying flowers.

My team met friends of a man who was missing. His friends placed his photo on a wall, while urgently trying to contact him by phone.

There were five teams to cover the areas where flowers had been laid, Monument Tube station, Borough High Street, The Embankment, the railway station and, of course, on London Bridge itself, where TV cameras were positioned. There were people

[98] 'London Bridge attack: What happened', 3rd May 2019, https://www.bbc.co.uk/news/uk-england-london-40147164 (accessed 6th July 2020).
[99] Chris has described his experiences as a Street Pastor in Chapter 8.

laying flowers, some just wanting to stand, cry and shake their heads in disbelief, asking, 'Why?'

On Wednesday we met a young man on crutches who had been there on the Saturday night. He was with a friend and told us how lucky he felt to be alive. We supported him as he told us a bit about his ordeal. He had been winged by the van.

As we continued to mingle with the crowds, we listened to their stories – where they had been on the night, how they had just left the area and reflecting on what might have happened if they had not moved on.

Late Wednesday we met a woman who told us she had seen the police retrieve a body from the river close to her home. We wondered if it was the missing man whose photo had been posted by friends the day before. Our fears were realised as the death of the man in the river was announced the next day.

We spent some time in London Bridge station talking to the staff. They were so pleased to see us. Some had been working on the night of the attack but were determined that the terrorists wouldn't win.

On Thursday, just one Response Pastors team of five people was deployed. By now, Borough High Street was fully open, but the Borough Market area was still closed as police continued with their work.

As we stood and mingled with a large group of people at the end of London Bridge, where the flowers were, a woman on her bike stopped. She sat on the pavement and just cried. One of the women in our team sat down with her. In time the tears dried up, smiles appeared, then laughter and huge hugs, and she climbed back onto her bike and rode off. Just sharing some love had made all the difference.

We picked up our bags and walked back over to the bridge down to the galleries for a coffee break. People were stopping to say hello, including a woman who asked if she could join us. She had seen us from the offices upstairs and wanted to pray for us and the work we were doing.

The last afternoon was spent at the end of London Bridge talking with those who wanted to tell their story. Then it was time to leave. The team hugged and prayed as we said our farewells. Sitting on the train heading back north, it began to sink in what I had witnessed and the stories I had heard. I thanked Jesus for the opportunity to stand with those in need.

Another member of the same team was Jan Ganney, who had served as a Street Pastor in Sutton for ten years and was a recently trained Response Pastor. She quickly responded to the appeal for volunteers and made her way into London, kitted out with her 'Go Bag' containing tissues, pen and notepad, bottle of water, disposable gloves, torch and pocket Bible and wearing her Response Pastor tabard and cap:

On London Bridge we spoke to passers-by. Many wanted to talk about their thoughts and feelings following the incident, which hopefully was therapeutic. Most people were surprisingly positive, thankful that they had not been a victim and wanting to carry on life as normal. One woman, out walking her dog, as she did every day, told us that she wasn't going to let fear stop her from going about her business.

I also spoke to a homeless man who was sitting on the pavement. He had been there when the incident happened but thankfully hadn't been injured. He said he had helped a pregnant woman and wanted to find out if she was OK. He had no credit on his mobile phone so I called the helpline to ask them. They said they would make enquiries and call him back. I thanked him for being brave and helping.

I often say that people shouldn't always have to make the effort to go to church because the Church should be going out to them. Being a Response Pastor is just that – the Church going out to the people.

Grenfell Tower

On 14th June 2017, a fire broke out on the fourth floor of a twenty-three-storey tower block called Grenfell Tower in North Kensington, west London. The small fire which began in a fridge freezer spread rapidly. Within two hours the whole building was ablaze. Seventy-two people died. Many others were injured.

Sixty-five people were rescued by the fire services. As there was a 'stay put' fire policy, many residents who sought safety in their flats perished as the fire spread out of control. The fire did not burn out for twenty-four hours.[100]

A Response Pastor remembers Grenfell:

The day after the fire, I travelled to Grenfell Tower with another Response Pastor. Approaching the area, we turned the corner and suddenly had a full view of

---

[100] BBC News, 'Grenfell Tower: What happened', 29th October 2019, https://www.bbc.co.uk/news/uk-40301289 (accessed 6th July 2020).

the building. We both stood still and gasped. There was this huge, ghostly black building towering overhead. It was such a shock, a truly awful sight. There was also the overpowering smell of smoke and burning.

We reported to a local church where people were handing out clothing and water, and joined the rest of the team for our briefing. I was one of six who had the honour of working behind the police cordon. This had never been allowed before, so we were rather hesitant. Crews from fire, police and search and rescue were there and had set up a forensic tent.

We introduced ourselves and gently allowed the crew members to talk as they wanted to. We didn't ask many questions unless it felt appropriate. You could tell the ones who had been there at the scene because they looked downcast, almost forlorn. One was a fireman in his early twenties who had just arrived from Australia and had been called out that fateful night.

'After Grenfell, my life will never be the same,' he confessed.

We were also introduced to the working dogs who were there to search methodically through what was left of the building, both inside and outside, for human remains – what a job.

To be honest, we didn't really feel like we did very much; we simply listened to people and let them talk. Interestingly, they opened themselves up more when their teammates were out of earshot.

At the end of our shift, the team leader came over to us and thanked us.

'You have no idea how helpful you have been to us today. We are all in shock but we don't show it; we put on a brave face. But you have come and listened and that has really helped,' he said.

The Manchester Bombing

Response Pastors travelled from north, south, east and west to support those affected by the terrorist bombing at an Ariana Grande concert in central Manchester in May 2017. Although a good 100 miles away from Manchester, Response Pastors from Chippenham, a historic market town in Wiltshire, made their way up north.

The following account is an article written by Stefan Mackley, printed in a Wiltshire newspaper, *The Gazette and Herald*, on 1st June 2017.[101]

Chippenham Street Pastors at scene of Manchester terror attack

Two Chippenham Street Pastors were called upon to use their specialist training and help grieving families, friends and the people of Manchester following last week's terrorist attack.

Michael Weeks, the co-ordinator of Chippenham Street Pastors, and Becky O'Brien, the headteacher of Marden Vale Academy in Calne, volunteered to go to the city last Wednesday and Thursday where they offered what support and help they could.

---

[101] Stefan Mackley, 'Chippenham Street Pastors at scene of Manchester terror attack', *The Gazette and Herald*, 1st June 2017, https://www.gazetteandherald.co.uk/news/15322441.chippenham-street-pastors-at-scene-of-manchester-terror-attack/ (accessed 4th July 2020). Used with permission.

Twenty-two people, including children, were killed when a bomb went off at an Ariana Grande concert at the Manchester Arena on Monday May 22. A further 60 people were injured.

Both Mr Weeks and Ms O'Brien have been trained as response pastors, which prepares them to help others in the event of a major incident, whether that is flooding or a terrorist attack.

'It was in the back of my mind whether I should go,' said Mr Weeks, who trained as a response pastor last year.

'I had a chat with my wife and she was supportive of my decision. She knows I have done the training.

'We were there to provide a listening ear and people were coming to pay their respects. If they wanted to talk, we talked. If they wanted a hug, we gave a hug.

'I can only use the word solidarity. Everybody is in it together.

'Everybody was really caught up in the tragedy. It was tragic.'

Mr Weeks led a team of 16 people, including street and response pastors from across the UK.

Street Pastors is a charity founded in 2003 and is made up of volunteers who take to the streets of cities and towns ensuring that their communities stay safe.

Ms O'Brien said: 'A month ago we had a training exercise in Chippenham, but I couldn't have imagined I'd be deployed so soon in such a tragic context.

'The national co-ordinators asked for support for the Manchester pastors.

'Our job is not to give advice but to take time to listen to people carefully, comforting them and standing alongside them as they process what has happened. We worked alongside emergency services, local clergy and religious leaders of other faiths.

'On Wednesday we were deployed in St Ann's Square, and there was a very subdued mood in contrast to the normal Manchester vibrancy.

'There was also a huge sense of solidarity and people standing together, and we got a lot of thanks from people for being there.'

Rail Pastors

Suicide, once a taboo subject, has devastating ramifications – an act of desperation which causes immense distress.

Sadly, in 2019/20 there were 283 suicides/suspected suicides on the overground rail network – an increase of twelve from the previous year. During the same time span, rail employees, the police and the public intervened in more than 1,881 suicide attempts.[102]

Rail Pastors is a response to the tragedy of suicides on the railways and is another initiative within the Street Pastors family. It came about after British Transport Police offered their support with one condition, that a patrol 'like Street Pastors' could be established in Barnet, north London, where on a stretch of the rail network there had been a high number of suicide attempts and fatalities.

---

[102] Network Rail, 'Suicide prevention on the railway', https://www.networkrail.co.uk/communities/safety-in-the-community/suicide-prevention-on-the-railway (accessed 7th July 2020).

In 2014 the Barnet team was set up, and in its first year it conducted thirty patrols and saved three lives. Interestingly, during the same year there was a 27 per cent reduction in crime on that route. It soon expanded its area of operation and now carries out patrols on the Great Northern Route – the line that runs from Potters Bar to Alexandra Palace.

Rail Pastors also act as a reassuring presence to passengers and are ready to help needy or vulnerable passengers on the station platforms. Like Response Pastors, they are experienced Street Pastors. They receive training in rail safety and security and emergency procedures, and undertake a Managing Suicidal Contacts course organised by Samaritans.

Rail Pastors is now well established in Reading (2015), Fife in Scotland (2016), Birmingham (2017), Essex (2018) and Cardiff (2018).

Rail Pastors works in partnership with Network Rail, which has a National Suicide Prevention programme. Network Rail also works closely with British Transport Police and suicide prevention experts, such as Samaritans. This collaborative approach results in much less trauma and heartache for all concerned.

One person with experience of intervening in potential suicides on the railways is Phil Norton, aged fifty-four, who patrols the route between Shenfield and Colchester. Phil was a Street Pastor before training to be a Rail Pastor.

He was interviewed by Alasdair Hooper for Essex Live, and here are some extracts from that interview.[103]

'Primarily we're here as volunteers to try and help the industry in suicide intervention, that's our primary goal … We're here to support the work of Samaritans, the Greater Anglia staff, British Transport Police, the Land Sheriffs – who are all doing their very best to keep people safe.

'We come as volunteers because we realise they are busy, or doing rail stuff, whereas we don't get other things coming our way.

… We use low-level interventional work, being a good listener, going over to the people who we think might be vulnerable.

'That might be somebody who is hanging around, or might be trying to avoid detection, or be hiding on the railway line.

'It's just trying to cheer them and to get them out of that cycle of, "I have no hope and I have no way to cope with what I'm going through in life."

'We're just trying to help where we can.'

In 2018, Greater Anglia staff carried out 46 suicide interventions across the network.

However, when the time comes to act it can be an overwhelming experience, as Phil found out when he had to make his first intervention.

---

[103] EssexLive, 'Meet the Greater Anglia rail pastor who helps prevent suicides on the railway', https://www.essexlive.news/news/essex-news/meet-greater-anglia-rail-pastor-2458090 (accessed 6th July 2020). Used with permission.

'The first one was here at Chelmsford, and it was a young lad who was just not coping with life,' he explained.

'He'd gone out for an evening with his friends, he was part of a group but something came over him.

'All the things he was going through in life – his life hopes, expectations, his career, his education – it just, for that moment and for a short period of time, completely overwhelmed him.

'He decided that was the time that he was going to take his own life.

'He came here to the station and it was very, very busy.

'Lots of Greater Anglia staff were on duty, lots of land sheriffs and police, and we had people here.

'Just using all those skills I have talked about, we became very aware that there was this young lad behaving slightly differently.

'So we kept our eye on him, we followed him and he went off the end of the platform and hid in the pitch dark at the end of the platform …

'We started to call out and fortunately after a short period of time he responded to our calls,' he added.

'He came back and then we just looked after him, we made sure he was safe, we got great help from the police and the Greater Anglia staff.

'We called in the mental health triage nurse who came and at that stage the parents had been made aware …

'Once we got over our shock and emotions we really realised it was rewarding to be there at the right time and [right] place …

'Because we all have a faith, we pray for each other and as we were gathering in and praying the freight train came through.

'It rumbled through, it was powerful and it really did hit us that this could have been a lot worse.'

School Pastors

School Pastors are trained volunteers based in and around the school community where they offer friendship and safety and provide care. Wearing their distinctive uniforms, they patrol school premises and over time become accepted as an integral part of school life.

This initiative started in 2011 and has spread to thirty-one geographic areas involving forty schools and more than 450 volunteers.

In order to become a School Pastor, each individual has to undergo enhanced Disclosure and Barring Service (DBS) checks and to complete specialised training, including thorough safeguarding procedures. Through working closely with the schools, the teams are made aware of the reporting structures and the relevant people to refer information to. Any disclosures of a safeguarding nature are to be reported to the relevant person and are done so immediately with a view to empowering young people to make the disclosure themselves.

School Pastors also build relationships with the local school and community to establish what some of the needs or areas of support are for the young people and the staff. They work together to support these areas, primarily by providing a positive listening presence and encouraging supportive role models to enhance the physical, mental and social well-being of the school community.

For the relationships between School Pastors and pupils and staff to succeed, integrity is a key factor. People need to feel the School Pastors are trustworthy. A School Pastor must therefore work hard to build trusting relationships. They can do this by sharing their own experiences, their own story and own opinion, where it is appropriate and only when asked. School Pastors share personal stories hoping to inspire, but not to preach or judge. The young person is then free to take the initiative to ask further questions.

Prayer is an integral part of the process. School Pastors pray before and after a session in the school. If the team feels it is appropriate to offer prayer with a student, in agreement with the school, the team can offer to pray using pastorally sensitive language. Training and awareness around this issue is provided as part of the preparation to become a School Pastor.

The national coordinator of this initiative, Bejoy Pal, recalled some stories that stood out to him. For example, a group of secondary students in Kent shared concerns about their mental health. The School Pastors knew of a fitness instructor locally who specialised in stress relief, anger management and anxiety control through exercise. Together the team funded and facilitated several sessions so the students could attend. When the students asked, 'Why do you do this?' they replied, 'Because we care for you.'

Bejoy also described how their friendly, caring interventions can have a ripple effect, benefiting the teaching staff. In another case, a student in a school in Derbyshire made a complaint that his teacher had struck him. After talking to a School Pastor, the student admitted he had fabricated the allegation because he held a grievance towards that particular teacher. The teacher was spared being unfairly disciplined and the real threat of losing their job.

In a different school, a headteacher signposted a student, struggling with anxiety and stress, to a School Pastor. Over time the School Pastor built a positive, trusting relationship with the student with the result that the student is now thriving.

Some School Pastors contribute to other aspects of school life by helping at breakfast clubs, leading assemblies and taking part in Personal, Social, Health Education lessons and creating spaces of calm where students can relax and find peace.

Feedback from the schools has been overwhelmingly positive, as expressed in the following quotes:

School Pastors have been able to build the trust and respect of both the students and staff in the school. We're happy to signpost students as an early intervention to School Pastors to tackle some of the issues around anxiety and loneliness. We have seen this improve confidence in our students through these interactions.

Headteacher

It's such an encouragement to our staff to know that there is a prayerful supportive presence walking around our school. We can feel the atmosphere changing when our School Pastors are in.
School chaplain

I knew it was a no-brainer and that our children would benefit immensely from the additional pastoral support the pastors would provide in the long term. We've got to the stage where we think, 'I don't know what we did before the School Pastors were here, because they just fit so well in our school community.
Headteacher

Response, Rail and School Pastors have all evolved from the original Street Pastors model. Sharing God's love, compassion and concern, there is great potential for reaching even more people in need in the years to come.

Chapter 11
Area Coordinators in England

Ascension Trust, the umbrella body for Street Pastors, grants a licence for Christian groups in different areas to set up and run Street Pastors, according to Ascension Trust's principles and training.

One of the conditions of setting up a Street Pastors group is that at least four churches of different denominations are working together. Different denominations of churches working together help with Church unity, ensuring that Street Pastors in an area does not become a 'project' of just one church, but rather reflects the broader Church. This allows churches of varying outlooks and styles to be involved, which adds to a richness of Street Pastors teams.

Behind the scenes, a lot of work goes on to make sure that individuals are suitably vetted, trained and in other ways equipped to serve the community as Street, Rail, School or Response Pastors, as well as in the setting-up of rotas, liaising with other organisations and more. This work falls to area leaders or coordinators.

While those living in the Greater London area can take advantage of Street Pastors training in London, run by Ascension Trust itself, training in London is not suitable for those living in the rest of the UK. This is partly because of the distances people would need to travel, but also because local courses can be streamlined to the neighbourhood needs.

As such, one of the roles of group coordinators, as part of an area management team, may be to put together and run training of Street Pastors in their area, based on Ascension Trust's national training programme.

Here, three coordinators from different parts of Britain tell about their backgrounds and roles.

Taunton

Adrian Prior-Sankey was involved in the launch of Street Pastors in Taunton in 2008. Adrian has been the coordinator since then; he also carries out leadership training for Street Pastors nationally.

As a former special constable, chair of the council's licensing committee and vice-chair of the door supervisor regulation body, Adrian wanted to use his experience of the night-time economy to benefit the community through Street Pastors. In 2017 he was awarded the MBE for his services to the town.

Part of his motivation for becoming a Street Pastor was also because, 'A friend involved in a local rugby club had his brother assaulted in the town with no provocation. Through the work of Street Pastors, I felt I could make a positive difference in my neighbourhood.'

Adrian works one day a week as coordinator, and describes his role: 'Someone who stands between Street Pastors and the various agencies that they partner with. These agencies include the police and other blue-light services, such as the ambulance service. We also work with the local authorities in whatever form they take; with charities, such as those that work with the homeless; mental health services and of course the churches, from which individuals volunteer to become Street Pastors.'

Part of Street Pastors training encourages individual Street Pastors to be aware of the area in which they serve as Street Pastors, which may then help them in serving the local community and individuals.

The river Tone flows through Taunton, giving the town its name. Taunton lies within the borough of Taunton Deane, which includes the town of Wellington and surrounding villages.[104] Taunton has been described as 'a pleasant Somerset town, with picturesque streets lined with many fine houses and buildings'. It is sheltered by the surrounding Blackdown, Quantock and Brendon Hills.[105]

Like most locations in the UK, Taunton is not without its problems. In 2017, Taunton Deane Borough Council's housing options manager commented that a new drug, known as krokodil, was causing problems within the town.[106]

---

[104] Travel About Britain, 'Taunton',
https://www.travelaboutbritain.com/somerset/taunton.php (accessed 8th July 2020).
[105] Ibid.
[106] Amy Cole, 'Taunton Deane Borough Council says rise in use of drug Krokodil in the town', *Somerset County Gazette*, 18th October 2017,
https://www.somersetcountygazette.co.uk/news/15603395.taunton-deane-borough-council-says-rise-in-use-of-drug-krokodil-in-the-town/ (accessed 8th July 2020).

Apparently the rise of legal highs, such as spice and krokodil, were contributing to growing homelessness problems in the area, because their effects were stated to be so severe, that they were resulting in clients being evicted.[107] Krokodil, also known as crocodile, has been described as 'The drug that eats junkies'.[108]

In 2017, a major police dawn raid operation arrested twenty-seven drug dealers across Somerset, mainly based in the Priorswood and Halcon areas of Taunton.[109] A significant number of weapons and class A drugs were seized in the operation. Chief Inspector Lisa Simpson commented, 'People shouldn't have to live in places where dealers freely sell drugs on the streets, in parks or in areas where children play, which is what was happening in Bridgwater, Glastonbury and Taunton.'[110]

In Taunton, there are about fifty Street Pastors, split about half and half between men and women. A team of Street Pastors patrols on a Saturday night and on other occasions such as A-level results night. The patrol includes both a walking tour and a safe space street café, offering free hot drinks and a listening ear.

---

[107] Ibid.

[108] Shaun Walker, 'Krokodil: The drug that eats junkies', *Independent*, 22nd June 2011, https://www.independent.co.uk/news/world/europe/krokodil-the-drug-that-eats-junkies-2300787.html (accessed 8th July 2020).

[109] Alice Simmons, 'The faces of the gang jailed for 72 years for flooding Somerset's streets with drugs', *Burnham & Highbridge Weekly News*, 16th October 2017, https://www.burnhamandhighbridgeweeklynews.co.uk/news/15598970.the-faces-of-the-gang-jailed-for-72-years-for-flooding-somersets-streets-with-drugs/ (accessed 8th July 2020).

[110] Ibid.

Adrian says, 'We also provide other patrols for our annual illuminated carnival and other big events, where we are particularly asked to look out for lost children. We run School Pastors at one of our local academies. In addition we operate two daytime schemes on housing estates with high incidences of social deprivation.'

As would-be Street Pastors in the Taunton area can't get to London for training, Adrian is also involved in setting up and running training programmes in Taunton which also serve the wider region. He says:

The management team of Taunton Street Pastors put together an appropriate training package, based on the Street Pastors' national training manual and student notes. The manual and notes are made available to different trainers, who adapt the material to the area as needed. The training we provide requires a commitment of between fifty to sixty hours.

In Taunton, we source trainers with impressive credentials. For example, the session on mental health has the chief operating office of MIND Somerset, the local mental health charity, working alongside the former director of adult Social Services, who both generously give their time free of charge. The police also help with training, making their input relevant to issues relating to the night-time economy.

For our first aid training we are really fortunate to have a paramedic who gives his time free. We also have an NHS PMVA (Prevention and Management of Violence and Aggression) team that delivers conflict training. This is done in appreciation of Street Pastors

159

helping to reduce its workload through the service we provide.

During the training, would-be Street Pastors also have two or three opportunities to observe Street Pastors in action, by coming out onto the streets for patrols.

A further role of coordinators is to keep a record of key aspects of the work that Street Pastors do. This can be encouraging for volunteers, and it provides important and useful information for other agencies, such as the police or homelessness charities.

Adrian here shares just a few of the many statistics he has gathered for Street Pastors Taunton in the eleven years since he started.

We have patrolled at night for about 30,000 hours, in this time picking up almost 20,000 bottles (which can be used as weapons) and cans, giving out about 4,000 pairs of flip flops and 800 wet wipes. In supporting the vulnerable and rough sleepers, we interacted with 2,355 rough sleepers, and engaged with 1,296 vulnerable people. We also gave out about 6,500 hot or cold drinks, food to about 1,200 people and administered first aid to 101 people. During this time period we sadly witnessed 228 assaults and have had to call 999 about 200 times.

Adrian concludes by telling of a moving incident that Taunton Street Pastors was recently involved in.

On a very cold night just before Christmas, our team was walking through the town, and was asked by a member of the public, 'Would you go to the town bridge where someone is threatening to throw themselves in the river?' By the time the team got there, the person was in the river. His girlfriend was hysterical.

Whether because of the cold or the mental state of the man in the river, he was not easily able to grab hold of anything thrown to him. The team leader for the night managed to remain composed and was able to speak calming words to the man. Soon the team was able to able to throw a lifebelt very accurately, and managed to carefully pull the man to shore. During this time the emergency services had been called, onlookers were kept at bay as far as possible, and other team members calmed the girlfriend.

The emergency services arrived quickly, but the first people on the scene who had a big hand in saving the man's life were the Street Pastors.

Plymouth

Plymouth, about seventy miles south-west of Taunton, has been associated with the Royal Navy since the late seventeenth century.[111] This is the city from which Sir Francis Drake set out to challenge the Spanish Armada in 1588, and from which the *Mayflower* sailed to America in

---

[111] Plymouth, Britain's Ocean City, 'The Royal Navy at Devonport', https://www.visitplymouth.co.uk/things-to-do/the-royal-navy-at-devonport-p1689703 (accessed 8th July 2020).

1620.[112] Now it is a busy city with a population of around a quarter of a million.[113]

Roy Beaumont coordinates a team of about eighty Street and Prayer Pastor volunteers in Plymouth. He says:

My role includes recruiting new volunteers, ensuring they are DBS checked and have uniforms, organisation of training courses and commissioning services for trained volunteers. I also organise the team rotas every six months, then send reminders to that week's team, with adjustment of rotas for people sick or on holiday. We organise extra patrols, for example, on Bank Holiday Sundays and Halloween at the request of the police.

I attend regular meetings with police, council, university, CCTV, Best Bar None,[114] Taxi Marshals, ambulance service and fire brigade and give talks, for example to churches and Women's Institute (WI) groups. Other duties include production of a newsletter and updating our website and more. One of the most rewarding parts of my role is hearing success stories, which I pass on to the team, to local churches and more widely, for their encouragement and information.

Also rewarding, in 2019, Plymouth was presented with Purple Flag status, an award given to cities and

---

[112] Ibid.

[113] UK population 2019, 'Population of Plymouth 2019', https://ukpopulation2019.com/population-of-plymouth-2019.html (accessed 8th July 2020).

[114] Best Bar None Plymouth, https://bbnuk.com/schemes/plymouth/ (accessed 25th July 2020).

towns that surpass the standards of excellence in managing their evening and night-time economy. The various organisations that presented to the assessors stressed that the unity between their groups, which include **Street Pastors**, was the main reason why the night-time economy worked so well.

Since **Street Pastors** started in Plymouth, here are just a few of our many stats.

We have given away about 8,500 pairs of flip flops and use about 700 bottles of water each year, either to wash wounds or to help rehydrate drunk people. We have removed more than 75,000 bottles from the streets and have given first aid to more than 450 people. With respect to possibly saving lives, since we have been operational, teams have been involved in resuscitating two people, helping avert eight suicides we know of, and saving at least three people from hypothermia.

Roy recounts one incident that really touched him, which, he said, 'sums up what we do in so many ways':

One night we came across a middle-aged woman collapsed in a side street, with three or four members of the public around her, trying to help.

As soon as they saw us, they called us over with some relief, saying, 'You'll be able to help her, won't you?'

We assured them we could, but it really spoke to me of the trust we have built up over the years, to the point where they were completely confident to leave her with us, which they did.

We started to try to rouse her, to find out her name, address, etc, but she was so 'comatose' that all we could get out of her was some unintelligible burbling.

Out of politeness, more than anything, we told her we would look through her bag and pockets to see if we could find some ID for her, or someone we could maybe call to come and help. There was no ID whatsoever in her bag or pockets. Hope was raised when we found her phone, and then dashed when we found it had no battery life, so we couldn't call anyone on her address list.

We turned to our secret weapon: we rang the Prayer Pastors for prayer. I must say it took over a minute, but the answer came walking around the corner in the form of two policewomen who knew not only the woman as a street sleeper, but also the hostel she was staying at. To our delight, they offered to radio for a van to take her there.

While we were waiting for the van, one of our ladies on the team that night began to cuddle her as a mum would, even in her drunken state. I watched the woman respond and snuggle into Angela's shoulder.

The van came and we helped her in, but she began to cry, looking at us. It was quite hard to watch as the door was closed. I don't know, but I like to think that through the tears, she was crying out for more of the affection she had just had and which, in all probability, hadn't had much of lately.

I've thought a lot about that incident and realised how much of what we do is summed up in that meeting, the trust of the public, the amazing answered prayers, the love given through what we do and the deep effect it has.

Reading

Reading is about 200 miles north-west of Plymouth, a historic university and minster town in Berkshire. It has a similar population to that of Plymouth[115] and, although it is near to London, it is a major commercial centre in its own right. Commerce in Reading includes information technology and insurance, contributing to more commuters coming into the town each day than those who leave it. In 2019, Oxford and Reading were rated as top-performing cities in the UK for the fourth year in a row.[116]

Like all cities, Reading is unique in many ways, including being home to a music festival with its origins in 1955, making it the longest-running music festival in the world.[117] During the August Bank Holiday each year, the festival attracts about 100,000 people. Many of the UK's most successful rock and pop bands have played at the festival, including The Rolling Stones, Fleetwood

---

[115] City population, 'Reading', https://www.citypopulation.de/en/uk/southeastengland/reading/E3500150 1__reading/ (accessed 8th July 2020).

[116] PWC (PricewaterhouseCoopers) South East, 'Oxford and Reading once again top Good Growth for Cities Index', https://www.pwc.co.uk/who-we-are/regional-sites/south-east/press-releases/oxford-and-reading-once-again-top-good-growth-for-cities-index-.html (accessed 8th July 2020).

[117] 'Reading and Leeds Festivals', https://en.wikipedia.org/wiki/Reading_and_Leeds_Festivals (accessed 8th July 2020).

Mac, The Kinks, Pink Floyd, Deep Purple, The Who, Cream and many more.[118]

Sally Leonard is coordinator for Reading Street Pastors. She has been in the role for nearly eight years and works full-time, with her salary paid by Transform Reading.

Sally has been a Street Pastor for nine years. Prior to her current role as coordinator, Sally worked as a social worker, specialising in substance misuse, and as a counsellor. She feels that 'God was preparing me for this role'.

There are currently more than eighty volunteer Street, Prayer and Rail Pastors in Reading. Referring to 2018, Sally says:

> This was a very busy year again for Reading Street Pastors. Apart from two teams going out every Friday and Saturday night throughout the year, we were invited back by South Oxfordshire Police for the fifth year to attend Henley Regatta during the late evenings, from the Wednesday to the Saturday night.
>
> This worked very well, with us being based at Henley Baptist Church in the high street. We were working in partnership with the police and the two night-time venues in the high street. We have already been invited back again by the police.
>
> We were also asked by Thames Valley Police to be out on the streets of Reading for A-level result night.
>
> Royal Ascot was another venue we helped at, following an invitation to be involved from Windsor

---

[118] Ibid.

Street Angels, and in one evening alone we gave out 350 pairs of flip flops.

Reading Festival has been a huge success for Street Pastors, and we have been involved helping out at the Festival for the last eight years. We patrol the campsite, but also have two tents on site, serving refreshments or as places where people can come to chill out.

This year [2018] we were open 24/7 from the Wednesday lunchtime to the Monday morning. About 30,000 festival-goers came into the tents, which were manned by a total of 125 volunteers, both Street Pastors and people from different churches in Reading.

One festival-goer commented on our Facebook site, 'Hi, I've just come back from Reading Festival and wanted to thank you guys so much for being so helpful and non-judgemental. Two of my friends needed help from you and we are honestly so grateful. You do amazing work.'

Freshers' Week was the next big event, and again the police asked us to be out on the streets of Reading for three extra nights. Freshers' Week was very well organised, as Reading university has 'Freshers' Angels', who come into Reading with the Freshers to look after them.

In 2018, Reading Street Pastors received two awards. One was the Area Commanders Commendation from Thames Valley Police. The second award was Volunteer of the Year award, from Pride of Reading.

In addition to arranging that, two teams are out every Friday and Saturday night, Sally is involved in similar background work to other coordinators, including buying items such as flip flops and lollies for the teams to take out with them. Sally also gets involved in the pastoral care of her team members.

One of the differences with Reading Street Pastors from many other groups is that it works with First Stop, which comes under Transform Reading. First Stop is based in one of the local churches in the centre of Reading and is run by enhanced care practitioners (advanced paramedics), with the help of volunteers. If someone is deemed to need a paramedic, instead of sending them off to A&E or calling an ambulance, they can be sent to First Stop. Wheelchairs are available to take people to First Stop if needed. Sally's role includes some management of First Stop.

Summarising her role in Reading, Sally thinks:

> God has really opened the doors for us in Reading. I have not gone looking for these extra events; they have come to us.
>
> It's great that people recognise what we are doing and want to use us. Thames Valley Police say that we are an integral part of Henley Regatta in the night-time economy.
>
> One of the many satisfying things I see in my role as coordinator is that there are more than forty churches working together with Street Pastors.
>
> Street Pastors is probably one of the few initiatives where all the different churches work together,

whether Catholic, Baptist, Church of England, Pentecostal or whatever. It's just fantastic.

Chapter 12
Area Coordinators in Scotland

Ascension Trust (Scotland) was formed in 2010 at the Scottish Parliament in Edinburgh.[119] It is managed by eight directors, who are all from different Christian denominations. These directors have a wide range of professional backgrounds which they use with others to 'develop and implement practical and effective strategies to transform lives, promote community cohesion and advance social justice'.[120]

Glasgow

Stuart Crawford is the current coordinator for Glasgow city centre Street Pastors. Although his role is said to be part-time, he says it tends to be a full-time job. Stuart was a teacher for twenty-four years, but chose to retire two years early to do something different. After he retired, the role of Glasgow city centre Street Pastors coordinator opened up.

Although Stuart was not trained as a Street Pastor when the coordinator role became available, he felt the

---

[119] Ascension Trust Scotland, 'About us',
https://scotland.ascensiontrust.org.uk/about-us/ (accessed 8th July 2020).
[120] Ibid.

role was an opportunity to make a difference in his community and something that God wanted him to do.

Stuart had worked as a Church of Scotland minister for several years, an experience which he felt would be helpful for him in this new role. He had also volunteered with Glasgow City Mission, to help with its night shelter for homeless men and women. 'The experience of helping with the homeless for three years was a catalyst that confirmed that I really wanted to work with those on the streets in Glasgow,' Stuart says.

Glasgow is the most populated city in Scotland and the fourth most populated city in the United Kingdom, with about 600,000 people living there in 2019.[121] It was reputed to have been founded by the Christian missionary St Mungo in the sixth century, when he established a church on the Molendinar Burn, which became the focus of a large community, from which the modern city of Glasgow is said to have emerged.[122]

Interestingly, the Glasgow Coat of Arms bears the motto, 'Let Glasgow Flourish'. This is a truncated version of the words: 'Lord, let Glasgow Flourish by the preaching of the word.' These words are said to have been part of a sermon preached by St Mungo.[123]

---

[121] Population UK, 'Glasgow Population',
https://www.ukpopulation.org/glasgow-population/ (accessed 8th July 2020).

[122] Undiscovered Scotland, 'Saint Mungo',
https://www.undiscoveredscotland.co.uk/usbiography/m/saintmungo.html (accessed 8th July 2020).

[123] 'Did you know? – Glasgow's Coat of Arms',
http://www.rampantscotland.com/know/blknow_flourish.htm (accessed 8th July 2020).

While Street Pastors in Glasgow operates in a similar way to Street Pastors in other locations, there are obviously differences, as Street Pastors groups adapt to the community they serve.

Street Pastors in Glasgow has 140 volunteers, to include Street Pastors, Safe Zone Pastors and Prayer Pastors (individuals who pray for the safety and well-being of the team and those on the streets). The Safe Zone, similar to the one that operates in Reading, is a place where intoxicated people can be taken to recover. It is staffed by Street Pastors and police officers and saves on the number of people needing to go to A&E.

Of the nights out, Stuart says:

We patrol from 10.30pm and break at 12.30am if we are not dealing with anything then. We then have a break for an hour, and then we are out until 4am, although sometimes that can stretch until 5am.

The night tends to be divided into two halves, in line with the rhythm of the city. We tend to find that in the first half, we have the time and opportunity to engage with many of the homeless and beggars who are sitting on the city streets. The second half of the evening is when we are beginning to encounter the out-spilling of the pubs and clubs, dealing with those who are over-intoxicated or separated from their friends, although we still engage with homeless men and women at this time.

Stuart tells a story of helping a reveller recently:

We met a young man who was visiting the city during the festive period. He had come out of a club quite drunk, had lost contact with his friends and didn't know what hotel they had booked into on arrival in the city.

We asked permission to check his wallet, to see if a door key card might give us a clue as to his accommodation, but with no success. However, we did notice his warrant card for the armed forces.

We tried calling hotels in the city centre area, but nobody recognised his name. He told us the booking might have been in a friend's name, so we phoned all the hotels again, but still with no success.

Eventually he decided he would stay anywhere we could find him a bed for the night, a next-to-impossible task during the festive period. We were almost running out of options and praying fervently when we were 'directed' to a budget hotel. Amazingly, a room was available. We called the number he had given us for his own phone. His friends that he had lost contact with and who had his phone answered. We were able to make arrangements to reunite him with his friends the next morning.

Later that day, when sober, he sent a text: 'I don't know what would have happened to me had it not been for the Street Pastors.'

Like Plymouth, Taunton and Reading, Glasgow Street Pastors runs its own training using qualified trainers. This includes trainees going out on two supervised patrols.

Training includes basic first aid, such as learning how to put people in the recovery position, how to perform CPR for someone who has stopped breathing and how to deal with wounds.

Glasgow Street Pastors reports excellent relationships with Police Scotland, door staff and the companies that employ them and with Glasgow City Mission, whose main role is to help the homeless.

'One of the most satisfying aspects of my role as coordinator,' Stuart explains, 'is being able to do the background work to release people to do what they want to do on the streets; seeing the excitement of people going out, being able to patrol and encounter and engage with people. It is also great to be able to pray for and with people on the streets. Every week our teams have spiritual conversations. One of the most difficult things, though, is seeing recurrent issues, such as people (mainly the homeless) who have very little self-worth and are prepared to take any substance, not concerned if they will wake up or not. We recently had to give CPR to someone who had taken street valium.'

Street valium is also known as 'Street Blues', 'Vallies', 'Scoobies' and 'Benzos'. It has recently been associated with a number of fatal overdoses in Glasgow. It is considered particularly dangerous, as the contents of the tablets can vary. Tablets can, for example, contain etizolam instead of diazepam.[124]

Stuart continues:

We do not have the same issues with knife crime in Glasgow as in other places, because legislation toughened up on knife crime in Scotland. Now the

---

[124] Scottish Drugs Forum, 'Warning issued over "street valium" in Glasgow as deaths increase', http://www.sdf.org.uk/warning-issued-over-street-valium-in-glasgow-as-deaths-increase/ (accessed 8th July 2020).

charges for anyone carrying a weapon in Scotland are really severe, we don't see the levels of violence in Glasgow we hear about in other places.

Over the ten years Street Pastors has patrolled in Glasgow, people report that there is a different atmosphere in the city centre; things have got better. Where Street Pastors are patrolling, the crime rate has been reported to go down in Glasgow.

It's not possible to give all the statistics of what we do, but for example, in 2018 we gave out more than 2,000 pairs of flip flops, administered first aid to 190 people, calmed about forty fights and a further seventy aggressive people. We also picked up almost 5,000 bottles and offered prayer to more than 300 people. About 1,800 people showed appreciation, and 443 were referred to our safe zone space.

Edinburgh

Moving on from Glasgow and travelling almost fifty miles to the east, we reach the capital of Scotland: Edinburgh.

Edinburgh was recognised as the capital of Scotland from the fifteenth century,[125] and is Scotland's second most populous city with about 520,000 inhabitants.[126] It is the economic leader of cities in Scotland, with net

[125] HISTORIC UK, 'Edinburgh', https://www.historic-uk.com/HistoryMagazine/DestinationsUK/Edinburgh/ (accessed 8th July 2020).

[126] Cliff Hague, 'The figures behind Edinburgh's growth over past decade are astonishing', *The Scotsman*, 24th December 2019, https://www.scotsman.com/news/opinion/columnists/figures-behind-edinburghs-growth-over-past-decade-are-astonishing-cliff-hague-1399018 (accessed 8th July 2020).

immigration into the city, a strong tourist trade and in recent years a growing university population.[127] Since 1947 Edinburgh has been home to the International Festival and Festival Fringe, the world's largest arts festival.[128]

Street Pastors in 2019 celebrated operating in Edinburgh for ten years. Andy Amour, a former police inspector for thirty years, has been coordinator of this group for about three years.

Street Pastors Edinburgh currently has teams going out every Friday and two Saturdays per month. The teams can be found in all areas of the city centre, such as the OMNi Centre, Cowgate, Grassmarket, Princess Street and George Street. At each location, the teams are involved in talking to and assisting people, to help them stay safe and happy, sometimes when they are at their most vulnerable.[129]

Andy gives some background of Street Pastors in Edinburgh:

> We started in 2009 as a small group of about fourteen Street Pastors. Initially we went out just a couple of Fridays in the month, with the support of the police and local authorities.
>
> Edinburgh city centre is a busy place in the night-time economy, so this is where we patrol. As a busy city, Edinburgh is a popular destination for weekend

---

127 Ibid.
128 Fringe, 'What is the Fringe?', https://www.edfringe.com/experience/what-is-the-festival-fringe (accessed 8th July 2020).
129 Edinburgh Street Pastors, https://streetpastors.org/locations/edinburgh/ (accessed 8th July 2020).

breaks and for stag and hen parties, as well as locals coming in and enjoying pubs and clubs in the city centre.

Since 2009 the initiative has grown to a team of almost sixty volunteers in 2020. We now patrol every Friday night and a couple of Saturdays every month. We hope to grow soon so we can be out every Saturday also.

As part of my career in the police, I used to police the city centre where Street Pastors now patrols. It was quite a transition from being on patrol enforcing the law to being on patrol caring, listening and helping as a Street Pastor. However, it's all about dealing with and helping people. The police is one solution, Street Pastors is a different solution, but it's all for the good of society and individuals.

We spend roughly half of our time with the homeless and about half of our time with the revellers. In our standard kit for the night we carry tea, coffee, soup and biscuits, which we give to the homeless. We also carry small blankets, hats, gloves and socks to hand out.

About once in every two patrols, we have to call for help for a reveller who is over-intoxicated or someone who is injured. However, rather than calling an ambulance, we call a private charity called Street Assist, a new initiative in Edinburgh. Street Assist comes out to help using decommissioned ambulances and takes individuals back to a centre with first aiders. If needed, they can take people to A&E. It's a service designed to take pressure off the local hospitals, and it works really well.

With respect to its volunteers, Edinburgh Street Pastors runs two training sessions a year. Like other areas, it sources local experts to help deliver the training, which is made available to other nearby Street Pastors groups in areas such as the Scottish Borders, Fife and Stirling.

As in other locations, they work alongside and with a number of other charities.

Andy says:

We work with charities such as Bethany Christian Trust, which helps the homeless in Scotland, and with Teen Challenge.

Teen Challenge is a Christian charity that provides help for young people (but not only teenagers) coming out of addictions. It works in multiple locations across the UK, with more than 500 workers made up from staff and volunteers. It also has six residential centres in England, Scotland and Wales, with three in Scotland.[130]

Often we are the first point of contact for people in need, and can refer such people to these other organisations for help as needed. We have excellent relationships with the local police, the council and local politicians. This is illustrated at our annual Street Pastors commissioning service, at which new Street Pastors are recognised. Representatives from the police and the local council attend and give a vote of thanks.

---

[130] Teen Challenge UK, http://www.teenchallenge.org.uk/about (accessed 8th July 2020).

Andy concludes with a story which took place in Edinburgh City Centre one winter's night:

It was a typical encounter and the story could probably have come from many other areas, but it is a great example of what Street Pastors are doing each night they go out, caring for those in need, often people who have fallen into difficulty by accident.

A particularly wet night was on the cards for the team; heavy rain had been falling all evening and it didn't look like it was going to stop any time soon. Still, these are the nights we often see people at their most needy, so the extra push needed to go out is worthwhile.

I was leading a small group. We were an interesting mixture: a retired doctor, a social worker, a student nurse and a retired police officer.

We had already had a number of encounters with the usual mixture of homeless, revellers and night-time workers and were about to head back to base for our break when I spotted some people in a doorway across the road. It was one of those times for a decision. Will I go over there and check it out, or just carry on back to base? I went for the first option.

The doorway was dark, cramped and stinking of urine. Huddled together to keep out of the constant rain were three figures – as it turned out, a couple and their four-year-old daughter. Street Pastors see many pitiful sights but this was sad indeed. How on earth does a small family end up like this? Safeguarding ran through my head. The bad planning by the couple had left them exposed, especially the child. This had to be resolved.

They were from a town 100 miles north and had come to Edinburgh by train to buy clothes. They had missed the last train home and were stranded. Oh, and I forgot to mention the dog too. Hotels had refused them. I could smell the drink as we chatted.

'We'll be fine here for the night and just get the first train back in the morning,' was their plan.

Not in my book. Leaving them there overnight would be like when the priest and the Levite ignored an injured man lying on the roadside, in the story of the Good Samaritan.[131] Some things you can't ignore or leave to others. This family needed to be cared for, not least because a young child was involved and couldn't be left there. Street Pastors would have to be the ones to do it. But sometimes, for a number of reasons, people just don't want to be helped, and this can be really frustrating for us.

The next hour was spent on the phone asking, negotiating, begging, being refused and pleading to get these souls to shelter. Every road seemed to be blocked.

'We can take them but not the dog.'

'No problem, but we can't take children.'

'If they're from another town, we can't accommodate them.'

The excuses rolled in before we started to make some headway with an out-of- hours provider. Just then, the dad decided he didn't want to cooperate any more. Disaster! How can you help people who don't want to be helped? Negotiations continued. Now I

---

[131] Luke 10:25-37. A Levite was a religious leader.

had to persuade him as well that he needed to find a place for them to stay.

The team rallied round. Hot drinks for everyone, kind and caring conversation with the family, showing the love of Christ by practical means. Our team conveyed the same message: 'We care about you and we want to help you.' And so there was a turning and change of heart.

Then a breakthrough; now they would accept help. When it seemed like we had exhausted all means, an answer to prayer. The social work department emergency duty team from the local authority would arrange and provide transport back to their home town. We also knew that Social Services would follow up and take appropriate action, if they considered there were long-term concerns for the child's safety. That is prayer answered.

And so the three souls, cold, wet and miserable, were taken back to the shelter of home. Sometimes the Lord allows us to be used greatly to bring glory to Him. This was one such night.

Chapter 13
From the UK to Antigua

In the next three chapters, Sue Shaw describes her experience of working for Street Pastors Antigua in the Caribbean.

From the UK to Antigua

Working as coordinator of a Street Pastors initiative in outer London, I was responsible for almost seventy volunteers, organising patrols for every Friday and Saturday night in a vibrant town centre. With three large nightclubs that between them could accommodate some 5-6,000 people, plus smaller pubs and clubs, every night out was guaranteed to be eventful. The town had a large student population as well as a theatre, cinema complex, numerous takeaways and restaurants.

As coordinator I would oversee the deployment of volunteers mainly using the internet, as almost every volunteer had access to email. I had regular contact with ten team leaders who met quarterly, and organised occasional specialised training events for all volunteers on Saturdays.

There were the inevitable last-minute alterations because of sickness but, on the whole, things ran smoothly. I imagined I would stay in post as I was approaching retirement age, when unexpectedly the opportunity opened up for me to go and support an overseas branch of Street Pastors on the island of Antigua in the Caribbean. For several months, because of long-term sickness the initiative had had no leadership.

This seemed like a wonderful way of using my experience and people skills. For more than thirty years I had worked for a wide range of charities, managing volunteers, working with victims of crime, and I had also worked briefly overseas teaching English. The combination of serving God overseas and using my charity work experience was a powerful attraction. The fact that people in Antigua spoke English and drove on the left-hand side of the road only added to the attraction.

Having only a vague idea where Antigua was located, I quickly found an atlas. It appeared as a minuscule dot among the Leeward Islands in the Caribbean Sea. Some friends helped me to find the office using Google Earth. It was amazing to zoom in on the corner of two streets, Redcliffe Street and Corn Alley, and see the Street Pastors office building.

I imagined Antigua would be like the lush tropical island featured in the TV series *Death in Paradise* (which is filmed on the neighbouring island of Guadeloupe). It was exciting to think I was going to work in a similarly beautiful part of the world.

I learned that Street Pastors Antigua and Barbuda was the very first international branch of Street Pastors. It had been launched in January 2007 with the support of the then Prime Minister, Sir Baldwin Spencer, and a cabinet minister, Hilson Baptiste. The government financed a part-time coordinator, provided a seven-seater minibus with costs included and made rented office accommodation available.

In common with all other Street Pastors initiatives, the Antigua branch began as a partnership of the Church, police and government forming an urban trinity, with the aim of helping to bring peace to the streets and of assisting people in need. I also discovered that Rev Les Isaac, the CEO of Ascension Trust, the Street Pastors' umbrella organisation, had a special interest in the work as he had spent the first seven years of his life living in Antigua before his family moved to the UK. He visited Antigua on a regular basis, sometimes joining in the patrol nights and meeting with members of the management team to encourage and inspire them.

The internet provided me with useful factual information. Along with its smaller neighbouring island Barbuda, Antigua became an independent state within the Commonwealth of Nations on 1st November 1981. At the time there was an estimated population of 80,000 including people from countries such as Jamaica, Dominica, Haiti, Syria, China and Guyana. By the time I arrived in 2017, the population had grown to 95,426.[132]

With the abolition of slavery and then the decline in the cane sugar trade, the local people wanted other ways to earn an income. Over time the island's economy grew

---

[132] Worldometer, Antigua and Barbuda Population, https://www.worldometers.info/world-population/antigua-and-barbuda-population/ (accessed 7th July 2020).

to rely heavily on tourism, and it began to promote itself as a luxury tropical escape with 365 beaches, one beach for every day of the year.

Tourism developed in the 1950s when the advantages of having an airport, and drier sunny weather for most of the year, put Antigua ahead of other Caribbean islands. In 2018 Antigua welcomed a total of 1,081,365 visitors, which included 268,949 visitors who stayed overnight, 792,873 cruise arrivals and the remainder arriving by yacht.[133]

I also discovered that church attendance in Antigua is high. Twenty per cent of the population described themselves as evangelicals.[134] Church denominations ranged from Pentecostal, Anglican, Roman Catholic, Methodist, Moravian, Church of Nazarene, Baptist, Wesleyan Holiness, Evangelical and Salvation Army, Church of God of Prophecy and a multitude of smaller independent churches. There are no official figures but William Dorsett, the chair of the Ecclesiastical Commission of Antigua and Barbuda, informed me 'we have on record approximately 400 churches', on average one church for every 250 people.[135] Brand-new churches also register with the government on a weekly basis.

I flew into Antigua on a Tuesday afternoon, the first week of September 2017 a few hours ahead of Hurricane

---

[133] 'Antigua logs over one million visitors in 2018', Jamaica Observer, January 21st 2019, http://www.jamaicaobserver.com/news/antigua-logs-over-one-million-visitors-in-2018_155149?profile=1373 (accessed 7th July 2020).

[134] http://www.operationworld.org/country/anti/owtext.html (accessed 7th July 2020).

[135] Quoted from an email dated 25th October 2019. Used with permission.

Irma. It was the beginning of the monsoon season in the Caribbean. I spent my first night lying wide awake listening to the hammering and pounding of the wind on a galvanised tin roof. It sounded like a giant trying to break in. When the storm had passed, I moved to more permanent lodgings and met the chair of the management committee, Pastor William Holder, who gave me an introduction to the initiative. He explained I would be joining a team on Friday night in the capital, St John's, and would be picked up around 9.30pm. I would just need my Street Pastors polo shirt and cap and a small torch.

As I prepared for the patrol, I anticipated the many tourists, worse the wear for drink, who would need support to return safely to their hotels or cruise ships. I imagined St John's would be full of trendy, sophisticated nightclubs, expensive restaurants and large entertainment venues. The reality, as I soon discovered, was rather different.

My first night out

At 10pm it was still warm and sultry. I made my way to Subway, the takeaway sandwich store situated on Redcliffe Street, just opposite the Street Pastors office. Inside the air-conditioned shop, three Street Pastors in uniform were waiting for me: George, our leader, Ava and Tracey. The staff had already prepared a large plastic tray with twenty sandwiches plus carrier bags filled with five cartons of soda, six bottles of water and a box of cookies. Apparently, Subway had been providing Street Pastors with free donations of food and drink since 2007.

I was most impressed and wondered if this was an idea to take back home.

Between us we carried the boxes over the road to the Street Pastors office, located on the first floor of a plain concrete building. We donned cellophane gloves and placed each sandwich in an individual plastic bag, with a cookie and a serviette. As we worked, knotting each bag before packing them into two backpacks, I asked the others about themselves and discovered that they'd all been working as Street Pastors for nearly ten years, since its inception in 2007.

Before we left the office, George prayed for the evening, asking for protection and blessings, then we walked slowly down one of the main shopping streets. The pavements were very narrow, hardly room for two abreast, and I had to watch my step as the road was uneven. As we neared the centre of town, competing sound systems blared out rap or reggae music, while men sat on low walls or steps listening to the cacophony while drinking from beer bottles.

Our first stop was a square piece of wasteland where in the gloom I could see an old jeep was parked. The front side window had been smashed and was covered over with a piece of cardboard.

'Brother Arthur!' shouted George, tapping on the back window. Slowly the car door opened a few inches and they exchanged words, then George slipped a sandwich and a bottle of water through the gap.

'That is his home,' explained the leader.

'His home? Gosh! What happened?' I asked.

'I've known him for years. He was a policeman. He had a house which needed a lot of work. He gave someone his savings to do repairs, but they ran off with all the money.'

I reflected on this sad story as we slowly walked to the fruit and vegetable market building. On the way, we met a woman standing alone looking at the screen on her phone. One of the team asked if she was alright and they started to talk.

'If you could have a conversation with God tonight, what would it be?' they asked her. I didn't catch the drift of her answer, but the question was certainly a thought-provoking one.

There was loud, throbbing dance music coming from an alleyway where people were lining the pavement opposite a two-storey red-and-white wooden building, a rum bar. Inside, some guys were playing snooker while outside others were playing a noisy game of dominoes on a high, bare wooden table.

There were a few women, dressed up with sparkly jewellery, strappy dresses and high-heeled shoes. Apparently, this was the main nightspot in the town, where local people would come for their night out. I wasn't disappointed, more surprised, that the night-time activity was confined to small venues. There was certainly no sign of any tourists. I was told that they would either have sailed away in the afternoon en route to another island or were staying in all-inclusive hotels located way out of town.

From the rum bar we walked down the alleyway, across the road and up the steps of the public market hall, where we found two middle-aged men sprawled on the landing together, one with white hair, the other with long dreadlocks, a bushy beard and a broken arm in plaster. By the state of their old and stained clothing, I guessed they were going to sleep here. They cheerfully accepted the sandwiches and water, the man with white hair eating his sandwich still lying out flat. There were tiny shards of broken green glass on the concrete floor, so I picked them up, as the guy with the broken arm had bare feet.

More men, poorly dressed, came up the steps to see what was going on and asked for food. Although I couldn't smell any alcohol, I later learned these guys were regular rum drinkers, rum being the national drink and relatively cheap to buy. We stayed chatting for a while then returned to ground level where we found a painfully thin and petite woman, wearing a glittery blue top, who was completely bent over at a ninety-degree angle, grasping a walking stick. She looked so frail.

'OK?' I asked.

She shook her head and said something incomprehensible to me. Although most people speak English, I was discovering that many speak a local dialect, Antiguan Creole English, which to my ears they spoke very fast.

From nearby, a plump woman, selling bottles of juice and soda from a rickety stand, brought over a rusty metal chair, the seat constructed from cardboard, and plonked it down. I steadied the frail woman so she didn't topple over as she dropped onto the seat.

A couple of Rastafarian guys came up to shake my hand, speaking in Creole. I had no idea what they were saying. My guess was that they enjoyed talking to someone with a British accent. One of them kept pumping my hand and with his other hand was beating his chest. Eventually I worked out that he was complaining that his windows had been smashed by Hurricane Irma, and he wanted to know what I was going to do about it.

A young woman approached us, looking very morose. The team recognised her and asked her a few questions. A single parent with two young children, she was struggling to find a job. We gathered round in a circle and George prayed earnestly for her.

Around half past twelve we made our way back to base, where our leader filled in a report form documenting how many people we had met, how many sandwiches we had given out, the names and, in some cases, the phone numbers of people we had spoken to, so they could be contacted later in the week.

'I wish we could do more for the homeless,' George said, with feeling. We all nodded in agreement.

'We feel the same in the UK.'

We finished in prayer, locked away the bags and made for home. It was 1.30am when I flopped into bed. Reflecting on the night, it was great there was the familiar outpouring of compassion and concern, especially for the more disadvantaged in society. But I hadn't expected that Street Pastors here would only meet local people; there hadn't been a single tourist in sight. I was also surprised that local men slept out all night on bare concrete floors. Nor had I been prepared for hearing people speaking in a local patois, which was incomprehensible to me. There were no door staff to chat with, no large-scale entertainment venues, no one obviously drunk and no long queues. It also seemed quite acceptable and easy here to talk about God, to pray openly. I had a lot to learn.

Chapter 14
On Patrol in Antigua

One week we were a small team – Annette, Brother Decastro and myself. It had been a struggle to contact volunteers. Compared to the UK, it was much more difficult to communicate with people. Only a couple of volunteers used email and sending letters was too unreliable, as most houses were not numbered. Even though many used mobile phones, I often had to leave messages and wait for people to return the call, which didn't always happen.

As normal, we bagged up the donated sandwiches and cookies. Headed for the market, we first stopped off at the jeep where Brother Arthur lived. He was awake, sat in the back seat, door ajar, and he had company. Two men were sitting close by on white plastic chairs, and a third, a guy with a bright multi-patterned shirt and long dreadlocks, stood talking. There was a strong smell of alcohol and a faint whiff of cannabis. We offered them sandwiches and everyone was happy to take some. We turned to leave.

'Wait,' said the guy with dreadlocks. 'I want to pray.'

We all bowed our heads and he prayed for us all. Then he asked me to pray, and I asked God to help us with the battles we all face, whatever they may be. Annette invited them to her church and they nodded politely.

Moving on, we climbed up to the first floor of the covered market area. Two dishevelled men were sprawled out on the tiles. One was fast asleep. We gave food and water to the guy who was awake.

Further along we found another four men, whom I now recognised, including the one with a broken arm and the older guy with white hair.

'How long before you can take the plaster off?' I asked.

'Another two weeks,' said his mate, grinning, revealing just two teeth.

'Do you have a home?'

He shook his head.

'Me mother no want me. Me father passed when I child.'

'Sorry to hear that,' I said, gently placing my hand on his shoulder. His eyes were red and rheumy.

'Me mother she bang me,' he said.

I was puzzled.

'He mean his mother, she beat him,' Annette interpreted for me.

'When me child,' he added.

'That is so wrong.'

'She bang me with a big stick.'

It was hard to know what to say. Any words seemed inadequate. The guy with white hair said nothing, and lay with a radio clutched to his chest, listening intently.

Meanwhile, Brother Decastro had sat down on the market steps with a young guy who was wearing a smart blue polo shirt with an embroidered monogram. He was staring at a photograph on his mobile, showing it to Brother Decastro. Tears were running down his face.

'His mother, she passed,' Brother Decastro explained.

The photo showed a young couple on their wedding day. The young man continued to cry, his shoulders heaving up and down. I knelt and rested my hand gently on his arm.

'You must have loved her very much.'

He nodded but couldn't speak.

'His mother died in the States. He couldn't go to see her,' Brother Decastro said.

With heads bowed and eyes closed, Brother Decastro prayed, asking God to comfort the man and give him peace. As we stood to leave, he remained clutching his mobile, staring at the old black-and-white image.

After giving out more sandwiches, we circled level one and came across three guys playing dominoes on a plastic folding table, noisily slapping down each brick with gusto.

One muscular guy in a tight, red, long-sleeved top had both ears pierced with big gold studs. He owned a nearby mobile phone shop, and knowing we were Street Pastors and Christians, he fired off some challenging questions. Did Pharaoh have a wife? What was the Passover? Who was the woman who attacked Samson? Why was it forbidden to eat pork?

His friend, dressed in baseball cap and navy boiler suit, asked even more-challenging questions. What did

Jehovah Witnesses believe? And Seventh Day Adventists? Why did they forbid jewellery and alcohol? Why didn't God forgive Lucifer?

We talked at length, finally agreeing that what's important is what is going on in the heart, not outward appearances, but loving God and others. The third guy shook his head. He thought lots of people who go to church were fake. The guy in red loudly disagreed with him.

Outside, on the far side of the fish market, we found another rough sleeper lying on bare concrete, huddled against a wall, exposed to the wind. There were lots of empty wine bottles strewn about. I knelt down beside him and offered him a sandwich and bottle of water. He lifted his head very slightly.

'You need some cardboard,' I said, and retraced my steps in search of a piece that I had noticed earlier. I slipped it gently under his head.

'I've lots of problems. You go.' He slurred his words.

'Do you feel safe?'

He pointed up to the sky.

'God is watching over you?' I surmised.

He nodded.

'Do you need anything?'

'Need some shoes, some underpants,' he mumbled, and pointed towards his feet. On his left foot he wore a black flip flop but nothing on his right foot.

'OK. What size?'

'Size nine.'

I made a mental note and promised to return on Monday. It was the first time I had been asked for flip flops. Back in the UK, Street Pastors freely give out flip flops, not to rough sleepers, but to young women who can no longer walk in their high heels after a night out dancing.

At home, in the night I was woken by the sound of a torrential rainstorm. I thought of the street sleepers, especially the man on his piece of cardboard, and prayed that they would find somewhere less exposed to sleep. Although many of the rough sleepers have relatives and often a home on the island, their drug and drink dependency issues often propel them to living outdoors. There are no official numbers for rough sleepers in Antigua, but they are numbered in their tens rather than hundreds.

The following Monday I bought a pack of five pairs of men's underpants from an outdoor stall. The vendor knocked the price down when he heard who they were for. Then I bought a pair of size nine plain brown flip flops from a Chinese minimarket and took them down to the market area. It was raining again. I found our friend sheltering round the side of the fish market.

'You weren't too well on Friday,' I said.

He nodded his head.

'After we left there was a big storm. Did you get very wet?'

'I went by the guys gambling,' he said, pointing to the back of the covered fish market where people often gathered at night to play cards.

I handed over the flip flops and two pairs of underpants. He grinned.

He shook off his one flip flop and pushed his feet into the new brown ones. They were a touch too small, but he was grateful. He stuffed the underpants into the pocket of his baggy khaki shorts.

'It was my birthday yesterday,' he told me, grinning.

'Fantastic! Happy birthday! I'm so glad I came today,' I replied.

Several months later, when I was back in the UK, I heard this man had died, alone, on the floor of the public market. I was so glad our encounter had been such a positive one.

The other side of town

One week we had a group of observers, young people from *Logos*, an international missionary cruise ship touring the Caribbean and South America. There were enough of us to break into two groups, the first to visit the market area, the second to go to the other side of town where there was a small street known for its red-light activity.

We headed north, past the police station, towards Popeshead Street where I was surprised to see several expensive cars with tinted windows either parked or cruising past. Three white Mercedes-Benz cars were lined up outside a strip club, a bright yellow building, where a few men were sitting on a narrow wooden bench on the pavement.

'How does the sex trade work here?' I asked Kenny, the team leader.

'The women are usually from other islands, not Antigua. They are probably trafficked and have to give all their earnings to their employers who provide food and accommodation,' Kenny explained.

'Are we allowed inside?'

'Yes. We can go in.'

We filed in through a narrow wooden door. Inside it was noisy, dark and almost empty. Neon lights flashed above the bar area. There was a strobe light throwing out coloured beams across the room. A solitary guy, baseball cap pulled down low, was swaying on the dance floor. He seemed in a trance. Several scantily clad women were either sitting at the bar or walking around talking to customers. A buxom woman in a black leotard was pole-dancing on a small platform. At the back of the room, an enclosed cabin with a window looked out on to the dance floor. Inside the cabin, two DJs were operating the sound desk.

It was too loud to hold a conversation, so I gave a thumbs-up sign to a woman seated at the bar on a high stool. Our observers had brought some Christian literature with them and handed out a sheet entitled 'The Father's Love' and some New Testaments. No one refused.

Back outside we gathered on the crazy paving. Some guys followed us out. One of them was a skinny young man in a red top with various gold chains round his neck and a colourful baseball cap which was on back to front. He was one of the DJs. Two of our team talked with him, while Kenny and I were regaled by a tall guy dressed all in black, a Rastafarian with dreadlocks that reached down his back and several long, gold chains hanging round his neck. He said he had come straight from a meal out with his workmates. He was passionate about Jah,[136] not cutting his hair, the Creator, wiseness (not wisdom). For a good hour we talked and listened.

'I spread wiseness,' he said, 'and joy. I am full of joy.' He grinned. He was missing some bottom teeth. He pulled out his hair band and shook his long locks. 'Just like a palm tree, man, like a palm tree.'

Kenny asked him some challenging questions, such as, 'Who made the Creator? What do you think about death?'

He had great respect for the Bible but was adamant that Rasta existed before Adam. He raised his voice and waved his arms around animatedly. During the conversation he disclosed that he was a grandfather, had four children and was widely travelled. Eventually another guy walked up to him and gestured for him to join him.

'Me a com,' he said to his friend. Turning back to us he said, 'Now me a go inside.'

We thanked him for talking, shook hands and gave him the sheet, 'The Father's Love', before he returned inside the club.

A new routine

After a few patrols I noticed that the team's energy levels were really flagging by midnight. When I mentioned this to one of the Street Pastors, they explained this was because people would often be up at five o'clock in the

---

[136] Jah means the Supreme Being of Rastafarianism.

morning to do their chores, before the temperature rose to the usual twenty-seven degrees Celsius.

Over the next few patrols, I checked with all the Street Pastors if they would prefer to start earlier. 'There's no law that says you must begin so late,' I explained. The new idea had unanimous support, so our starting time moved earlier, to eight o'clock. This meant we also met a wider range of people and had more conversations, especially with the rough sleepers, as many had often fallen asleep by half past ten.

It was still our custom to saunter along the dimly lit side streets greeting passers-by, taxi drivers and vendors, wishing them 'goodnight'. It had taken me a while to realise that saying goodnight was the traditional way of greeting people, whereas back in the UK I would say 'goodnight' not on meeting but when leaving after spending time with them.

Deliberately moving slowly, we stopped to chat and gave out sandwiches, all the while heading for the centre of town where we knew many of the rough sleepers gathered. We would walk by the American-style burger bar, the small *shawarma*[137] takeaway, past the street vendors at their wooden stands grilling corn cobs, chicken legs and stuffed shellfish over hot coals.

We would speak with one particular vendor, Sami, often dressed in a colourful bandana or shirt, who had set up a trestle table on the pavement close to the rum bar where he sold single cigarettes, slices of raw tobacco, incense sticks, a few cosmetics and swigs of rum from an

---

[137] A Middle Eastern dish.

opened bottle. He had quite a busy trade. He chatted to us with ease, often complimenting us on our work.

Near the centre of town, with dance music belting out from enormous speakers, the road was often jammed with cars crawling along bumper to bumper.

We passed by the casino, a dimly lit room filled with flashing slot machines, where we could peer inside. Tellers wearing smart uniforms dished out plastic chips to the punters sitting on high stools, transfixed by the screens. It was only when the customers stepped outside the front door that we could chat to them.

Dotted around the edge of the bus station were small, brightly painted sheds where men played cards, slapped down dominoes or watched a flickering TV screen. There were guys sitting on wooden benches playing Warri (meaning 'house'), a traditional game using wooden balls like marbles that rest inside twelve wooden hollows. We didn't interrupt their concentration but waved and smiled as we wandered by.

Close to the town centre supermarket, a couple of televisions had been set up on tables by the roadside so people could watch a DVD, often an action film or thriller. Several men watched from the other side of the road, sitting down on the pavement or leaning back against the railings. We would greet them by bumping fists. There was never any animosity or criticism or name-calling.

Not by bread alone

As was our custom, we visited Brother Arthur, the older guy who lived and slept in the old jeep.

'Brother Arthur!' shouted our leader, tapping on the side window. Slowly the car door opened a few inches. They exchanged words and the leader slipped through a sandwich bag and a bottle of water.

'Still reading your Bible?' he asked.

'Yes, brother.'

'Do you need anything?'

'Something to read,' he replied.

Over the next few weeks, we left him different paperbacks – a crime thriller or a spy novel – along with a sandwich and some water. Then one night we found the land empty and Brother Arthur sitting on a low wall with all his belongings stacked around him – four or five bags and a small cardboard box. He was wearing fawn suede workmen's boots, a dark T-shirt and trousers and a navy baseball cap. I could see his features more clearly: shiny skin, thin angular face, black-framed glasses.

'What's happened?' I asked.

'They've taken de car away.'

'What are you going to do?'

'Me waiting for a friend from de force. Me going to stay by him.'

'Where does he live?'

'In town.'

'That's good. We've brought you some books.'

I handed over a novel, a book about the history of Street Pastors and a New Testament. He was especially pleased with the New Testament.

'See you again.'

'Me be back. You see me,' he assured us.

A few weeks later we heard the sad news that Brother Arthur had died. Thank God that Street Pastors had made it a priority to visit him every patrol.

Chapter 15
Looking Back

Keeping people safe

One of the first questions people often ask when they hear there is a Street Pastors branch in Antigua is, 'Is it safe?' It is difficult to find actual crime statistics for Antigua but there are news reports and personal anecdotes about robberies, thefts and burglaries.

Serious crime such as murder is usually within local communities. In 2017 there were twenty homicides, an increase from eight the previous year. Of these twenty cases, twelve were solved.[138] The police believe most were drug-related crimes and involved repeat offenders. Compared to other Caribbean islands, these are relatively small numbers.

During my time on the island I did not witness any crime, though I was told various stories. One night we did meet a man wielding a long-barrelled gun, but we discovered later that he had confiscated it from a troublesome customer outside his bar.

---

[138] 'Police to take a stronger stance on crime in 2018', *Antigua Observer*, 9th January 2018, https://www.antiguaobserver.com/police-to-take-a-stronger-stance-on-crime-in-2018 (Accessed 6th July 2020).

Long-standing Street Pastors provided me with the following examples of crime-related incidents or times when they helped people to keep safe.

A man carrying an illegal firearm asked Street Pastors to escort him to the police station, where he handed in the gun.

A wanted criminal asked Street Pastors to support him as he had decided to give himself up to the police. A Street Pastor contacted the Police Commissioner and spoke to the family. It was agreed that Street Pastors would meet him in a deserted area and take him to the nearest police station, where he surrendered himself without any problems.

Street Pastors provided clothes and food for a family who lost everything when their wooden-built home burnt down.

At three o'clock one morning, the team met a heavily pregnant woman walking out on her own. She wanted to reach another town, so the team drove her there. Arriving at the address, no one answered the door, so they phoned her father but he refused to help. Eventually they took her to a safe place in a different area.

Very late one night, the team met a woman with a baby and a toddler. She told them that she was planning to sleep out under someone's veranda. Street Pastors asked how they could help. She explained that her landlord had thrown her out as she hadn't paid her rent. Street Pastors phoned her boyfriend who said he couldn't help her financially, even though he was earning. They next spoke to the landlord and pleaded with him to allow her to stay just for the weekend, which he agreed to do. The next week the coordinator Sister Pat followed up and happily her boyfriend had agreed to pay the rent.

A young man, during an argument, was attacked by his own father who was wielding a cutlass, a long-bladed knife normally used for cutting long grass. A Street Pastors team leader managed to calm the father down as he was about to kick his son. He persuaded the father to let his son collect his clothes, his passport and some belongings. The young man asked Sister Pat to keep his passport safe in the Street Pastors office until he needed it.

A man came out of a nightclub and began talking with the Street Pastors who were standing outside. He asked them, 'What are you doing here?' The conversation developed and the man began sharing his life story. He became very emotional, breaking down in tears, with his nose running. A Street Pastor embraced him. Before they parted, the man pulled out a long knife and admitted that before he met the Street Pastors team, he had been on his way to murder somebody.

Drugs

There are severe penalties if people are caught dealing hard drugs, but this does not prevent drug-taking.

Cannabis is popular and crack cocaine is available, but as it is more expensive fewer people use it.

Street Pastors are not there to judge but they do try to encourage the users to take better care of themselves and to seek help. Sadly, some of the habitual drug users end up in long-term psychiatric care. During my time in Antigua, two street sleepers we knew well were found dead because of sustained drug use. However, we could refer people to substance abuse support groups that met regularly in different places on the island and to a residential rehabilitation centre in Antigua called the Crossroads Centre, founded in 1998 by rock legend and recovering addict Eric Clapton.

Crossroads, a luxurious complex of residential and therapy rooms, is set in landscaped gardens overlooking a beautiful turquoise bay in the far south of the island. The fees are high and it attracts wealthy people; however, subject to an assessment interview and medical testing, some local people are offered free places.

Over the years, Street Pastors has been involved with many men and women with drug or alcohol dependency issues, and here we introduce two of them.

Meet two guys

JoJo
Jojo jumped up to greet us. An intelligent man who often enjoyed a serious discussion, this night he slurred his words.

'Me take cannabis heavy,' he admitted.

'God wants you to know He loves you,' said one of the team.

'God wants you to have a better life than this,' I added.

'How?' he asked. 'I need go to hospital. Need brain scan.' He turned his face away from us. I recalled that Jojo had told us on a previous occasion that he suffered with seizures, and this worried him.

'God loves you,' I repeated.

'God took me dad. He had cancer. They give him five years, but he had another twelve,' he almost growled.

'You're angry with God for taking your dad?'

'Yes!' he exclaimed.

'Was it a sudden death?'

'Yes,' he snapped. 'I'm going to cry,' and with that he strode off into a dark corner.

Inadvertently, I had touched a raw nerve.

JoJo returned a minute later and began to apologise.

'No need to apologise. God understands your anger. He understands how you feel,' I said.

'Pray for me?' he asked.

We all stood in a huddle, arms around each other's shoulders, and prayed for him. Before we left, I reminded Jojo that nothing, not even our anger, can separate us from God's love.[139] As I walked away, I couldn't help wonder if his cannabis addiction was related to unresolved grief and anger.

---

[139] See Romans 8:38-39.

Gem

Gem originates from another Caribbean island and moved to Antigua many years ago to live near a close relative. When Street Pastors first met him, he was sleeping out every night on a piece of cardboard laid on the concrete floor in the entranceway to a public building. Gem had long dreadlocks piled up on his head, swathed in a black cloth. Quietly spoken and very courteous, he was one of a small group of regular rum drinkers.

Street Pastors frequently stopped to speak to him and his friends and to give out water and sandwiches. One day he took the initiative to visit the Street Pastors office and he bravely asked me for support to go into rehabilitation.

I arranged for him to have an initial assessment interview at Crossroads and drove him down there. Gem was considered to have the right motivation and attitude and was offered a free place on the one-month-long residential course, plus a six-month stay in a halfway house.

Within a few weeks, Gem had a starting date. Sister Pat and I collected him with his possessions, meeting him in a quiet part of town to preserve confidentiality, and drove him to the centre. He agreed that we could visit him during his month-long stay, so we returned to visit him on a couple of Sunday afternoons. He told us that he was finding it very challenging and sometimes uncomfortable. But he also acknowledged that attending daily group meetings, talks about health and well-being plus one-to-one counselling sessions were beneficial.

Eventually Gem left Crossroads, and he spent the following six months in a halfway house, sharing with other former Crossroads guests. There he received ongoing support until he was able to live independently. Gem now has paid work and lives in his own rented home. No more bedding down in the open on a sheet of cardboard.

Making a difference

In all, I spent eighteen months in Antigua and was privileged to witness many lives being transformed thanks to the intervention of Street Pastors.

During that time two men began to attend a local Alcoholics Anonymous group for weekly support. At first, one of the men was very reluctant to join because his clothes and shoes were shabby. Wayne, a Street Pastor, found him some smart trousers, a T-shirt and a good pair of leather lace-up shoes so he was able to participate with his head held high.

Towards the end of my time there, we met a woman who was a regular drinker; we had prayed for her several times. She was wearing a sparkly green top and a baseball cap pulled low over her eyes, and was sitting on a low wall. We exchanged words and I complimented her on her manicured toenails. She raised her head and looked me straight in the face, with a big smile. 'I've given up the booze,' she said proudly. This woman had been drinking heavily for well over thirty years.

When the street sleepers were all moved away from public buildings by security guards, Street Pastors were determined to find them. It took a while to work out that they had relocated to sleeping under a shipping container situated on waste ground. Nonetheless, we continued to deliver the sandwiches and bottles of water, in the process developing trusting and friendly relationships with several men.

Before I left to return to the UK, we were approached by a local secular charity called Adopt a Family.[140] It had established a soup kitchen in a refurbished container on the same wasteland where we had originally met the late Brother Arthur in his jeep.

Adopt a Family had started to provide hot food and a drink three times a week at lunchtimes for anyone in need, and asked Street Pastors to become involved. Now, once a week and on special occasions, Street Pastors Sister Camelda or Brother Barry, my successor, cook and serve a large tureen of nourishing soup for up to sixty people.

As well as a good example of partnership working, the soup kitchen provides an opportunity to engage with many of the same people to whom Street Pastors distribute sandwiches and water on Friday nights, as well as others on a low income. It also shows Christians following the example of Jesus who 'came to serve, not to be served'.[141]

As I reflect on my time in Antigua, I recall the inspiring words of the former Archbishop of Canterbury, Rowan Williams, who said, when talking about the story

---

[140] 'Adopt a Family in Antigua and Barbuda (Help us)',
https://www.globalgiving.org/projects/adopt-a-family-in-antigua-and-barbuda-help-us/ (accessed 7th July 2020).
[141] Mark 10:45.

of the widow who put a small coin in the temple collecting box,[142] 'You don't have to make every kind of difference, but you do have to make the difference that only you can make.'[143]

I have tried to make a difference that only I could make. I have helped individuals such as rough sleeper Kevin who, after he fell and broke a hip, spent several weeks in hospital where I visited him. Months later, although back out sleeping on the streets, Kevin had put on weight, no longer needed to use a walking stick, and was going to church.

I am also encouraged by the words attributed to a prayer said by Spanish Carmelite nun Saint Teresa of Ávila (1515-82):

> Christ has no body now but yours. No hands, no feet on earth but yours. Yours are the eyes through which he looks with compassion on this world. Yours are the feet with which he walks to do good. Yours are the hands through which he blesses his world.[144]

I'd like to end with the words of William Dorsett, chair of the Ecclesiastical Commission of Antigua and Barbuda, which acts as a bridge of communication between the many diverse church denominations and the government. William told me:

---

142 See Luke 21:1-4.

143 Rowan Williams, 'No One Can Be Forgotten in God's Kingdom – TEAM Conference, South Africa', 9th March 2007, http://aoc2013.brix.fatbeehive.com/articles.php/1436/no-one-can-be-forgotten-in-gods-kingdom-team-conference-south-africa (accessed 6th July 2020).

144 Teresa of Ávila, quotes, https://www.goodreads.com/quotes/66880-christ-has-no-body-now-but-yours-no-hands-no (accessed 6th July 2020).

The Street Pastor is the only hope that some persons can access in their greatest time of need. Encouragement and guidance to a better way of life is valuable. Through the years, Street Pastors have been filling a void and we are grateful for this shepherding on the streets of our nation.[145]

---

[145] Quoted in an email dated 25th October 2019. Used with permission.

Chapter 16
Safety on the Streets

Sarah Williams, an experienced Street Pastor trainer, specialises in safety issues. Here she describes some of her personal experiences on the streets alongside issues that she covers in the safety training modules that she delivers to Street Pastors around the country.

After hearing a talk about the ministry of Street Pastors, I realised how important it was for me to express my faith in a practical way outside the four walls of the church, so I applied to be a Street Pastor.

As I love to see others develop and grow, I also took the opportunity to become a Street Pastors trainer, working with both new and current Street Pastors. I have been doing this for several years. It helps that I am an active Street Pastor and when training can quote real-life situations so that people give me feedback such as, 'You can tell she has walked the walk.'

Safety on the streets of our towns and cities is paramount for both Street Pastors and all who venture out onto the streets, whether they are celebrating, drowning their sorrows or working through the night. As Christians, Street Pastors believe God's presence is with us, but we do need to be prepared for possible accidents and potentially dangerous incidents.

For example, while on patrol one night we saw several lads run down an alley that led to a busy road. One lad ran straight into the road, maybe in his haste forgetting it was there, and unfortunately was struck by a moving car. He was badly injured, sustaining a broken leg, but we knew how to support him until the paramedics came and took over. When the ambulance drove off, leaving the friends behind, we were able to reassure them and listen to their concerns for their friend.

An important safety practice is having a minimum team size of three Street Pastors. This allows one person to deal with the situation, another to contact the Prayer Pastors team and/or the emergency services if needed, while the third person can be fully engaged in observing what is happening on the streets, technically known as 'situational awareness'.[146] This is particularly vital when the streets are full of people fuelled by alcohol or other substances, as events can change rapidly and the team needs to be on constant alert.

Each team has a team leader or senior, and an important part of their role is to make sure the team stays safe. Another important safety point is for each team member to keep eye contact with all other members of the team throughout the night. This ensures no one gets separated from the rest of the team. In the event of separation, which can occasionally happen, sometimes in error and sometimes as a result of an incident, then a

---

[146] Mica R Endsley and Daniel J Garland, *Situation Awareness Analysis and Measurement* (Bosa Roca, FL: CRC Press, 2000).

prearranged meeting point should be agreed. This could be the operating base if it is close to the patrol area.

Dealing with conflict

There have been several occasions on patrol when it looked like a fight was breaking out. In these cases, a phone call to Prayer Pastors has resulted in things calming down, or if a fight was in progress, it would de-escalate rapidly.

Where there is the potential for a fight, we often use lollipops as a distraction tactic. One night we came across a group of lads who were showing 'warning signs' of aggressive behaviour, which could easily have escalated into something more serious. I grabbed a handful of lollypops and held them out, loudly saying, 'Lollies!' The lads, in surprise, repeated, 'Lollies!' and they each took one and were so busy unwrapping their lollypops and enjoying eating them that they completely forgot about the fight.

Fights do occur from time to time, so it is important that the team remains safe. When confronted with a fight, the team must maintain a safe distance using the knowledge they gained on training about 'interpersonal space'.

There are four categories that distinguish the amount of space between people. The intimate distance of one centimetre to forty-six centimetres is appropriate for embracing, touching or whispering, and normally people are invited into this zone. The personal distance applies to interaction between good friends and family members and measures between forty-six centimetres and 120

216

centimetres. What is known as the social distance applies to acquaintances standing between one and four metres, and finally the distance for public speaking is four to eight metres.[147]

For Street Pastors, much interaction is in the personal distance space, but we also move between this and the intimate and the social distances. When a significant incident occurs, Street Pastors need to move quickly to the social distance where the potential swing of an arm or a fist will not impact them.

Alcohol consumption removes the awareness of these social conventions. The intimate space is frequently entered into without an invitation, and those who are alcohol-fuelled often are completely oblivious that they have entered this intimate zone.

'Warning signs' of potential violence can include postures such as holding one's head high, facing one's intended victim of attack with arms spread wide and a darkening in facial colouring.[148]

'Danger Signs' include a side-on pose with fists raised above waist height, dropping the head and lowering eyelids as a means of protection. If this sign is demonstrated, the safest place is definitely at least two metres away.[149]

Whenever 'warning signs' change to 'danger signs', Street Pastors must move away to a social distance.

---

[147] Edward T Hall, *The Hidden Dimension* (USA, NY, Bantam Doubleday Dell Publishing Group, 1988).
[148] Care Certificate Training, 'Recognising Danger Signs', https://www.procarecertificate.co.uk/training_video/recognising-warning-signs (accessed 8th July 2020).
[149] Ibid.

Experience has shown that praying on the street is very powerful, particularly when there are no other visible resources. From a safety point of view, when praying as a team or even when praying with someone, it is still important to maintain 'situational awareness' on the streets. Therefore, it's a good idea for the whole team to keep their eyes open while they are praying.

Alcohol issues

On any one night, a good number of people on the streets will have consumed various amounts of alcohol and some will have taken other drugs. It can be a very tough call to judge whether to phone for an ambulance or not. Street Pastors must discern if there is a risk to life and then act in accordance with this assessment.

False alarms happen when people are not fully aware of different levels of alcohol intoxication and how they affect people's actions. Sometimes an ambulance can be called when it is not actually required. There are times when the paramedics arrive on the scene and the intoxicated person is already up and heading for another club. So great wisdom is required to avoid wasting precious time when the paramedics could be dealing with a more urgent case.

One night we were called to a male who was sitting slumped on the pavement outside the main club. He was unable to communicate properly or stand up. Police and paramedics had attended, neither felt their area of expertise was required, so it was over to us as Street Pastors. The team felt a little abandoned, but we stayed with him and eventually he was able to get up. Once he had done this, he started to weave his way up the road, watched over by CCTV. Had we been better informed of the process of alcohol intoxication, we might not have called for police and paramedics. Alcoholic intoxication is measured from one to seven levels as below:[150]

1. 'Sobriety, or subclinical intoxication' – no particularly obvious outward manifestations of intoxication. The blood alcohol content (BAC) is likely to be about 0.01 to 0.05 per cent.

2. 'Euphoria' – an increase in chattiness, delayed reactions and decreased inhibitions, among others (also known as 'tipsy'). BAC about 0.03 to 0.12 per cent.

3. 'Excitement' – loss of judgement, visual problems, loss of balance and drowsiness, possibly nausea and vomiting. BAC about 0.09 to 0.25 per cent.

4. 'Confusion' – may black out without actually passing out, they forget what is happening around them and may not feel pain. This group are at a high risk of injury. BAC about 0.18 to 0.30 per cent.

5. 'Stupor' – the inability to walk or stand, when they may pass out or have seizures and may lose control of bodily functions. They will need immediate medical attention. BAC about 0.25 to 0.40 per cent.

---

[150] Sunrise House, American Addiction centres, 'What Are the Stages of Alcohol Intoxication?', https://sunrisehouse.com/stop-drinking-alcohol/stages-intoxication/ (accessed 7th July 2020). Paraphrased except for headings. Used with permission.

6. 'Coma' – this is a dangerous state, with slowed breathing and sluggish circulation, loss of motor function, loss of gag reflex and a drop in body temperature. BAC about 0.35 to 0.45 per cent.

7. 'Death' – generally occurs with a BAC of 0.45 per cent or above, but death can also occur at lower levels.

When coming across a person who is intoxicated it is not a matter of fitting them into an exact level, but monitoring them as to whether they are going up or down the scale. This can take some time, so it is wise not to rush off to deal with another situation. A rough rule of thumb practised by the emergency services is that if the person can walk and talk then they may not need help at that point in time. Things can and do change very quickly, however.

An example of the euphoria level is when a young man asked if he could marry one of the team. Another night a lad suddenly said, 'What do you have to do to get a date with a Street Pastor?'

One of the team replied, 'Go to church.' Everyone laughed.

Is it safe to give water to someone who is very drunk? This is a question often asked when a lot of fellow drinkers want to persuade their mates to drink water.

The NHS guidance for helping someone who is suspected as having alcohol poisoning is as follows:

- try to keep them sitting up and awake
- give them water if they can drink it

- if they have passed out, lie them on their side in the recovery position and check they're breathing properly

- keep them warm

- stay with them[151]

It should also be considered that several conditions can mimic alcohol intoxication. These include low blood sugar or hypoglycemia, traumatic brain injury, some stroke symptoms such as slurred speech, decreased cognition and altered gait, later symptoms of encephalitis, advanced sepsis and others. Several drugs such as benzodiazepines, barbiturates and others can also mimic alcohol intoxication.[152]

One night on patrol we came across a young lad who was definitely showing signs of intoxication, or so we thought. However, several people we talked to reported that they had seen him fall and hit his head, which was important information for the paramedics.

On another patrol, when it was exceptionally cold – a team member's phone stopped registering the temperature at minus nine degrees centigrade – we noticed a man wrapped round an advertising hoarding, dressed in nothing more than jeans and a smart shirt, so we presumed he was drunk. The paramedics attended

[151] NHS, 'Alcohol Poisoning', https://www.nhs.uk/conditions/alcohol-poisoning/ (accessed 8th July 2020).
[152] Joe Bennett and Hilary Fairbrother, 'Alcohol Intoxication Mimics: ED DDx + Approach to Management', emDocs 30th August 2017, http://www.emdocs.net/alcohol-intoxication-mimics-ed-ddx-approach-management/ (accessed 8th July 2020).

and quickly whisked him off to hospital, as his core temperature was very low. A few days later we met up with the paramedics and they reported that if he had not been found when he was, he would not be alive.

Drug issues

Any team out will have noticed an increase in the smell of a variety of drugs being smoked or vaped around areas of their town. Teams may also find a lot of small, silver nitrous oxide canisters strewn around, or see someone using a balloon to consume nitrous oxide (laughing gas). Teams will also hear stories of spiked drinks or drug snorting. The consumption of illicit drugs increases safety concerns. Whether drugs have been knowingly taken or they have been slipped into a drink by a fellow reveller, this is another serious consideration for patrols.

One night the Street Pastors team was called by CCTV to a female lying on the ground and not responding. It quickly became apparent that the paramedics were needed. While the paramedics dealt with the female, the team formed a human wall to protect the woman from passing cars getting too close and interested bystanders who wanted to get involved. Her drink had been spiked and her safety was our highest priority.

Recreational drugs fit into three main groups, with a fourth having been added more recently. These groups are: downers – central nervous system depressants; uppers – central nervous system stimulants; and mind changers – hallucinogenics. In addition, the synthetic cannabinoids are treated as a separate category, not fitting neatly into any of the other three categories and in relation to their clinical management.[153]

On the street we come across people who have taken club drugs that cross all these classifications. Club drugs are commonly used recreationally, taken to feel different, rather than a drug of dependency. According to a 2018 BBC article, in the UK, cocaine is the second most widely used drug after cannabis, followed by ecstasy/MDMA, then ketamine, followed by amphetamines.[154] Ecstasy and cocaine would be widely considered as 'club drugs'.

The details below of different illegal drugs that might be used in the night-time economy are brief. For more information, please read the referenced source material.

Downers or depressants[155] [156] [157]
Drugs classified as downers include benzodiazepines which are tranquillisers, such as Valium and Xanax (street names such as vallies and benzos); the UK's most widely used illegal drug cannabis (dope, ganga, skunk, weed); GHB (G, GHB, gina, blue verve) which is also

---

[153] Novel Psychoactive Treatment: UK Network – NEPTUNE, 'Guidance on the Clinical Management of Acute and Chronic Harms of Club Drugs and Novel Psychoactive Substances', http://neptune-clinical-guidance.co.uk/wp-content/uploads/2015/03/NEPTUNE-Guidance-March-2015.pdf (accessed 8th July 2020).

[154] Jon Waldron and Prof Valerie Curran, 'The drugs being used at UK festivals', BBC News, 5th July 2018, https://www.bbc.co.uk/news/uk-44482290 (accessed 8th July 2020).

[155] Ibid.

[156] Black Bear Lodge, 'Is it Really Dangerous to Mix Uppers and Downers?', https://blackbearrehab.com/blog/is-it-really-dangerous-to-mix-uppers-and-downers/ (accessed 8th July 2020).

[157] Frank: honest information about drugs, https://www.talktofrank.com (accessed 8th July 2020).

commonly referred to as 'club drug' or 'date rape drug'; heroin (smack, skag), ketamine (K, ket, kit-kat) which medically is an anaesthetic and a powerful analgesic; subutex or buprenorphine, used to treat heroin addiction; and nitrous oxide or laughing gas. These react to slow the body down, having a direct effect on the heart and lungs. This group of drugs reacts when used with alcohol and the risks faced are vulnerability, lack of coordination, suppressed breathing and possible unconsciousness.

The issue of vulnerability is particularly a cause for concern because users can feel friendly towards anyone, which means they might become a victim of predatory behaviour.

Uppers or stimulants[158][159][160]

Uppers include amphetamines (speed, whizz); methamphetamine (crank, crystal meth, glass, ice) which is part of the amphetamine family; cocaine and crack (blow, coke, sniff, snow, white), the second most widely used drug after cannabis; ecstasy (dizzle, E, mandy, rolex) which is a popular club drug; mephedrone (bounce, miow, white magic) which can be compared to

---

[158] Ibid.

[159] Novel Psychoactive Treatment: UK Network – NEPTUNE, 'Guidance on the Clinical Management of Acute and Chronic Harms of Club Drugs and Novel Psychoactive Substances', http://neptune-clinical-guidance.co.uk/wp-content/uploads/2015/03/NEPTUNE-Guidance-March-2015.pdf (accessed 8th July 2020).

[160] Black Bear Lodge, 'Is it Really Dangerous to Mix Uppers and Downers?', https://blackbearrehab.com/blog/is-it-really-dangerous-to-mix-uppers-and-downers/ (accessed 8th July 2020).

cocaine and ecstasy; and amyl nitrate or poppers (liquid gold, ram, TNT).

A few of the symptoms that can be witnessed in someone who has consumed an upper may include violent behaviour with repetitive actions and speech, restlessness, high energy levels. People who have taken uppers are more at risk of assaults and getting into fights.

Mind changers

Mind changers or hallucinogenics such as LSD disrupt the senses and change how anyone taking it sees the world.[161] If they say they can see pink elephants, then they really do see pink elephants. Mixing mind changers with alcohol may make individuals 'more likely to be reckless, to harm yourself, or to endanger the safety of the people around you'.[162]

This can endanger Street Pastors and anyone else out on the streets. People who have taken any of these drugs experience an altered sense of time and space, loss of motor skills, an increase in heart rate and a feeling of detachment.[163]

New psychoactive substances such as synthetic cannabis

New psychoactive substances are drugs designed to replicate the effects of illegal substances like cannabis,

---

[161] The Recovery Village, 'What Happens When You Mix LSD and Alcohol?', https://www.therecoveryvillage.com/ecstasy-mdma-addiction/alcohol-acid-danger-mixing-alcohol-lsd/#gref (accessed 8th July 2020).
[162] Ibid.
[163] Ibid.

cocaine and ecstasy while remaining legal – hence their previous name 'legal highs'.[164]

Synthetic cannabis or cannabinoids are smokeable drugs with street names such as spice, black mamba, annihilation and Amsterdam gold. The synthetic chemicals are mixed with or sprayed onto herbs, typically on an industrial scale.[165]

More than eighty compounds had been reported in Europe by 2013, and the variability of the compounds means some are more potent than others. It has been reported that synthetic cannabinoids have been found in products that look like cannabis resin, as well as in samples of herbal cannabis.[166]

To complicate things further, synthetic cannabinoids can be mixed with other drugs such as benzodiazepines and phenazepam.[167]

Many studies have highlighted the adverse effects of the synthetic cannabinoid spice, such as altered mental status, anxiety, panic, psychoses, catatonia, seizures and more, including, in some cases, death.[168]

---

[164] DrugWise, 'Promoting evidence-based information on drugs, alcohol and tobacco', https://www.drugwise.org.uk/new-psychoactive-substances/ (accessed 8th July 2020).

[165] Novel Psychoactive Treatment: UK Network – NEPTUNE, 'Guidance on the Clinical Management of Acute and Chronic Harms of Club Drugs and Novel Psychoactive Substances', http://neptune-clinical-guidance.co.uk/wp-content/uploads/2015/03/NEPTUNE-Guidance-March-2015.pdf (accessed 8th July 2020).

[166] Ibid.

[167] Ibid.

[168] Rajashekar Reddy Yeruva, Hema Madhuri Mekala, Meesha Sidhu and Steven Lippmann, 'Synthetic Cannabinoids – "Spice" Can Induce a

If a drug from the depressant group has been taken, there may be a risk to the person, and so you need to deal with the person who has consumed the drugs. A Street Pastor would deal with this in the same way as they would with someone who has consumed alcohol.

On the other hand, if a stimulant has been taken, then the situation needs to be monitored as there may be the added risk of violence and aggression. For example, one night the team saw a lad running over the top of cars and then smashing the windows of a nightclub. This was definitely a situation for the police. On another occasion, a lad suddenly ran down a hill, leapt in the air and, as he did so, kicked out. His foot struck another person's head and then the assailant fell. His head hit the ground and he needed care for a head injury.

In the case of hallucinogenic drugs, each case needs to be assessed on an individual basis, always bearing in mind, 'Expect the unexpected'.

Conclusions

At all times, the safety of the Street Pastors team is paramount and should be considered in all situations. If the team can't solve the problem, they should not add to it by putting themselves in danger. Our aim is to be able to leave someone in a safer position than when we first met them, and for them to be safe from sources of harm.

As Street Pastors we know God is present, already out on the streets before we even venture out. Nevertheless,

Psychosis: A Brief Review', *Innovations in Clinical Neuroscience*, 16(1-2), 2019, pp 31-32.

Street Pastors need to be vigilant and wise as they go about their night-time duties.

Chapter 17
Prayer Pastors

Within the Street Pastors family is a group of people called Prayer Pastors who make a specific commitment to support the teams by praying while the Street Pastors are out on patrol. There are no special qualifications for this other than being an active member of a local Christian church that is or could be a member of Churches Together in England,[169] being willing to undertake some training, and ideally able to be physically present with the Street Pastors at their base.

Nobel Peace Prize winner, the late Mother Teresa, spent most of her life working as a nun and missionary in India. When talking about prayer, Mother Teresa said:

> Prayer makes your heart bigger, until it is capable of containing the gift of God Himself. Prayer begets faith, faith begets love, and love begets service on behalf of the poor.[170]

---

[169] Churches Together in England, https://www.cte.org.uk (accessed 16th July 2020).

[170] Mother Teresa Quotes on Faith, https://www.christianquotesbro.com/Mother-teresa-quotes-on-faith.html (accessed 6th July 2020).

For Mother Teresa, prayer and service were intrinsically linked. For her, prayer was not a substitute for action. After many years' teaching, she felt called by God to leave the security of a girls' convent school to care for the poor who lived on the streets of Calcutta.

Her work began with just twelve and grew into Missionaries of Charity, a worldwide movement dedicated to serving the most vulnerable in society, the poorest of the poor. The charity runs orphanages and AIDS nursing homes, and it cares for refugees, disabled people and victims of floods, epidemics and famines.[171]

Jesus, too, integrated his prayer life with service, meeting the myriad needs of people around Him. In the early years of the Church we read in the book of Acts how the disciples gathered for times of prayer[172] and set up a fund to care for widows.[173] The apostle Paul prayed faithfully for all the new young churches springing up,[174] but he also made every effort to visit them in person.[175] When people pray sincerely for others it naturally leads to action.

When the disciples asked Jesus to teach them to pray, His response was the Lord's Prayer.[176] He did not provide a list of rules, but by His teaching and example

---

[171] Mother Teresa of Calcutta, 'About the Missionaries of Charity', https://www.motherteresa.org/missionaries-of-charity.html (accessed 14th July 2020).

[172] Acts 2:42; Acts 4:23-31.

[173] Acts 6:1-6.

[174] Ephesians 1:15-20; Philippians 1:3-11; Colossians 1:3-14; 1 Thessalonians 1:2.

[175] Acts 14:21-23; Acts 18:18-23.

[176] See Luke 11:1-4.

He encouraged people to be real, to pray honestly and sincerely to a Father who already loves His children. As revealed from Jesus' stories of the Good Samaritan[177] and the Prodigal Son,[178] God is a loving heavenly Father who will respond to His children with mercy and compassion.

Praying to a loving heavenly Father is integral to the Street Pastors movement. People pray for wisdom, protection and whatever the Street Pastors need to be effective and make a difference to the people they serve. Prayer Pastors will pray for the people Street Pastors meet, for incidents happening on the streets and for the people who work through the night, such as door staff.

Usually they stay in contact with the Street Pastors team while they are on patrol through phone calls. They keep a log of calls and incidents and pray for real-time situations.

They welcome the team back with refreshments after each shift, and at the end of the night they join in the debriefing and pray. This is the ideal arrangement but, as locations vary all over the country, some Street Pastors initiatives have adapted this model to fit in with their specific situation.

We have already heard examples of answered prayer in stories from Street Pastors initiatives around the country. One initiative in Kent has provided the following story of how one Prayer Pastors team made a remarkable intervention:

---

[177] See Luke 10:25-37.
[178] See Luke 15:11-32.

One night, when I was a new leader, my team went out, supported back at base by a lovely Prayer Pastors group. On this particular night, the prayer team were vibrant and very connected with all that was happening. As normal, we phoned to tell them what we were encountering to help them as they prayed and worshipped together.

Partway through the evening, the team phone rang and the team member who picked up the call relayed to me that the prayer team felt very strongly that we should stop what we were doing and wait to see where God wanted us to go.

As the team leader, I first thought, 'Aren't I supposed to be the one directing here?' But I also knew it was important to accept their guidance. As we stood at a busy junction on the pedestrianised high street, I directed the team to split and stand and watch what was going on, and pray that God would show us where to go next. I was praying in earnest, 'Lord, show us, please.'

Directly across the high street from where we were standing was a narrow alleyway. Looking over, we slowly became aware that there was someone slumped at the back of the alley. The alley looked about ten to twelve feet deep and was full of old pizza boxes and who knows what else. We crossed over.

If I said it smelt like a men's urinal that would be doing men's urinals a disservice! It was so foul-smelling I had to fill my lungs with fresh air before entering the alley so that I wouldn't want to vomit.

Inside the alley, on a pile of pizza boxes, we found a young man, completely 'out of it'. We managed to wake him and retrieve his phone from the pocket of his skintight trousers in order to raise a contact for him.

Eventually we were able to move him away from the smelly alley onto a bench where he could tell us the code to activate his phone. We worked hard to keep him awake so that he didn't become unconscious through the effects of the alcohol and whatever else he might have taken.

After some time, his phone rang and we were able to speak with a friend. This friend told us that the man we had found, Brian, was meant to be staying with him in his student accommodation. As we helped Brian to walk with a Street Pastor on each side holding him upright, the friend agreed to come and find us. We had many quizzical looks from passers-by.

Eventually Brian was united with his friend and we delivered them both to the student accommodation. Before we left, we gave the friend instructions about how important it was not to leave his friend alone in case he vomited.

As I look back on this story, it shows me how much we are dependent on God to guide us. Through the prayer team, God asked us to stop and we obeyed. In stopping when and where we did, we found the young man. It is also a lovely illustration of how invaluable our prayer teams are.

A similar account of depending on God comes from an experienced team leader from Jersey in the Channel Islands who one night accepted the challenge to be a Prayer Pastor for a change:

At first, it was all very familiar and comfortable as I met with the team for their usual preparation, Bible reflection and outgoing prayer at the beginning of the patrol, but when the door shut behind them, I was the one left at base with the telephone.

Then it suddenly struck me that it was me who the senior on duty was going to call, and I would be the one tasked to pray into a situation. Suddenly, I was gripped with anxiety that I was not really a 'proper' Prayer Pastor and I was worried that I wouldn't find the right words, that I would let the street team down along with the people they were with, because my prayers would not be good enough.

As a senior, I knew how confident I felt when I phoned in a prayer request, knowing that the Prayer Pastor on the other end of the phone would intercede for me and the team. Now, however, I wondered if I had made a terrible mistake.

Yet, as the night wore on and the calls came, I was gently reminded that the power of God and the work of the Holy Spirit is not dependent on me, nor is it the eloquence of my prayers that enables God to be at work. I am involved in a partnership simply because God the Father loves to hear from His children.

I am slightly embarrassed to admit that I did not expect to encounter God so powerfully that evening, and I would encourage everyone to spend one night as a Prayer Pastor.

Some teams are supported by Prayer Pastors who pray from their own homes and keep in touch with events on the ground by regular phone contact. In some areas the prayer team at base sends text messages to the home prayers' mobile phones. In turn, those praying at home send back text prayers and encouraging messages to the base team, who relay them to the team out on the street.

Home-based Prayer Pastors are just as involved as those based with the teams, as illustrated by the following story from Sally Noel, the Prayer Pastors coordinator in Jersey:

At home one night I was Prayer Pastor covering the 1am to 3am shift. In the space of about forty-five minutes, the team on patrol made three significant calls asking for prayer. The first concerned a young lad in his late twenties who had an addiction to gambling. He had lost half a million pounds and was looking for a way to change his life around. The second call was about a young couple who had lost their baby the year before and were still feeling emotionally scarred. The third call was asking for prayer for a guy who had HIV. He had recently had a stroke and was feeling alienated and rejected by people, including his own doctor.

It was so challenging and touching to hear the depth of pain and hurt from people just passing by. I prayed for them and their situations, that God would cover them with His love and protection.

For the next few days, I was reminded of the young man with the gambling addiction, as our local radio station featured an advert for Gamblers Anonymous. I'd pray that he was listening to the radio and would have the courage to call them for the first step into changing his life around. For me, a Prayer Pastor's job is never just when we are on our assigned duty.

Georgia, a Prayer Pastor working from her Jersey home, describes how the role has affected her:

> The work has changed me and my attitude to people who choose to be out late into the night, whatever the weather. The night-time economy is complex and definitely isn't all it seems. Under the skin of many of the revellers is a deep searching for something or someone to make them feel better. I can feel the compassion radiating off the teams and it translates to me as sincere love for one's fellow men and women. I willingly do my part to carry them in prayer to God.
>
> Each night I was on duty I felt a deep connection to the team. It was as if I was charged with a power that would be hard to describe to anyone who has not been asked to focus on specific prayer requests over several hours.

Some initiatives, particularly in rural areas, may not have designated Prayer Pastors but instead they may have the prayerful support of local churches. Even where there is no organised prayer support, it is important to remember that Street Pastors out on patrol can also be prayerful as they walk the streets.

Prayer Pastors are made up of people from a variety of prayer traditions. Some people prefer to pray spontaneously, others like to use written prayers. Whether we pray aloud or silently, prayers are offered to God, who wants to hear what is on our hearts and minds.

In some areas there is a Prayer Pastors coordinator whose role is to keep in regular contact with the Prayer Pastors by mail, by phone and by meeting in groups or one to one. Keeping people informed and joint social events with Street Pastors helps to sustain a sense of teamwork and mutual appreciation.

After a patrol night, it is common practice to circulate prayer requests, thanksgiving points and stories either by email or in a newsletter to encourage interest in the work and stimulate prayer in local churches. As needed, the names of individuals are removed or changed, to respect confidentiality.

Prayer Pastors are required to abide by a code of conduct agreeing to high standards in areas such as transparency, integrity, conflicts of interest and respecting differences in custom, cultures and beliefs. This is similar to the code that is required to be followed by Street Pastors in order to preserve the highest standards in areas such as accountability and confidentiality.

The umbrella body, Ascension Trust, has four national prayer coordinators who provide prayer training materials, facilitate Prayer Pastors training nationwide and organise Prayer Gathering Days to encourage and inspire.

Their long-term goal is to develop a culture of prayer, where Street, Prayer, Response, Rail and School Pastors, along with coordinators and trustees, are united in depending on God for direction, provision and protection in each initiative.

Chapter 18
Responses, Awards and a Study

As we draw near to the end of the book, we consider some responses to the work of Street Pastors from individual members of the public who have been helped, and some endorsements from the police. We will also look at a few stories that have made it into the press, mention some awards and finish with a small research study about the work of Street Pastors.

These represent just a small snapshot of thanks, endorsements, press stories and awards.

Thanks from the public

General thanks[179]

You do a wonderful and heart warming job. Thank you for keeping us safer.

Thank you Street Pastors for being there, I feel 100% safer.

---

[179] Plymouth Street Pastors, 'Some Thank Yous', https://streetpastors.org/locations/plymouth/street-stories/some-thank-yous/ (accessed 8th July 2020).Used with permission.

I would like to thank you for the wonderful work you do. You helped us last night get reconnected and took us to the taxi rank xxx. I tried to give you a donation and none of you would take it, how can I do this as you really are lovely people?

On Saturday night just been I was saved by your organisation and I am so grateful. This is merely a token of the thanks I feel. I hope your work continues and would love to volunteer with you. [Message received with an online donation.]

Hi – I went out last night and lost my phone and I know I was being cared for by some Street Pastors as I was ridiculously drunk. I just want to express my sincere gratitude to whoever looked after me in my state, and I also want to apologise for being that drunk. Whoever looked after me were absolute angels, so thank you so so so much.

I would like to thank you all for taking care of me last night when I collapsed … I haven't been out for a drink with the lads since my stag night 7 years ago and I was unfortunately well out of practice.

You all cared for me so well. You were probably with me for an hour or so as I was in a right state. Thank you all so much. I don't know what would have happened if you were not there to look after me. My wife is also very grateful to you all. Thank you again and my upmost sincere apologies for getting myself into that state.

Just want to say a massive thank you to the gentleman and two ladies who walked me home. They were all so welcoming and nice and as well as walking me to my door, they warned me of potential risks of walking home at night, some of which I wasn't at all aware of. Again, thank you all so much, what you do is amazing and it doesn't go unnoticed x.

Good evening, I just wanted to say thank you very much for looking after me last night. Thank you so much for making sure I got home safely.

Just want to thank the lovely team that were working last night. They helped me get my keys and phone in order for me to get home. Couldn't have done it without them, keep up the good work.

Hi. I would just like to say a huge thank you to the 4 lovely street pastors who stayed with me until my partner arrived to pick me up last night. My friends were freezing, so I told them to go on as I wasn't feeling too well. Not drink I might add. I had an upset tummy. My friends were reluctant to leave me, but the pastors assured them they would stay with me which they did. I totally admire the work you all do and thank you very much again xxx.

What a fantastic service you provide. Helped the Mrs out last night and wouldn't take my money, so had to donate this morning. Great charity run by even better people. Many thanks.

Thanks from parents

Thank you so much for taking care of our son on Saturday evening. I know you spent a great deal of time with him and we are very grateful that you were there for him. Please find enclosed a small donation towards the great work that you do. Thank you again. God bless you all.

[A Street Pastor writes] During a patrol we spent some time assisting a woman till her mum came to collect her. Mum was great and got a taxi to collect her daughter. On the Sunday evening I got a text which said, 'Hello, this is N's mum. You kindly called me this morning to inform me that N was drunk and needed to come home. I just wanted to say thank you very much for looking after her and waiting until I got there. She is fine now and it's all thanks to your help.'

I am writing to say thank you, which seems such small words for what the Street Pastors did for my son. In the early hours of Sunday morning I had a call from a Street Pastor to say my son had been found drunk and very worse for wear and alone. They stayed with him, looking after him without judging him until I could get to them. Then they helped us get a taxi home. Please thank the woman and the two male Street Pastors who took the time to help us and I'm sure many others in the same way that evening. Having spent just a short time with them I witnessed their kindness and dedication to what they do.

I would like to thank [the Street Pastors] for helping my son one night when he'd drank [sic] way too much and was in a bad way until we got to him to get him home. If it wasn't for them helping him, giving him water and keeping him going, I think he would have ended up in hospital, which wastes the nurses' and doctors' time. They do amazing work out there. I think the hospitals should also be pleased, as they help to keep a lot of drunk people out of hospitals. Thank you so much.

First aid or ambulance calls

I will be eternally grateful as four years ago I was knocked unconscious on North Hill and left there. The Street Pastors suddenly appeared, put me in the recovery position and called an ambulance.

Thank you Street Pastors – you saved my friend's life – he got glassed and the only people that came to his aid were you.

Hi there, on Saturday night I was taken to hospital in an ambulance that was called by the Street Pastors. I have no idea who they were, but just simply want to thank them so much. They helped me out while I was unconscious, they kept me warm, safe and called the ambulance to help. Without them being there the night could have been far worse. Thank you so much.

I would like to thank the Street Pastors who helped me with my friend last night. Luckily she's now on the mend, as doctors think that she had a reaction to the alcohol which caused the stomach pain. Your assistance with supplying a poncho, blankets and water was much appreciated. Thank you so much.

Flip flops thanks

I am incredibly grateful to the Street Pastors ... last night who provided me and my friend with flip flops when our feet had completely given up in our heels. I know it's very minor in the fantastic work you do, but I cannot tell you how happy it made me at that moment in time. Angels! Thank you for the work you do.

[A Street Pastor writes] Recently we were approached by one young lassie who said she had been helped some months previously. Yes it had to be with flip flops. She had been drunk, very drunk. She had got extremely cross and angry about 'our' God, that what we believed was all rubbish etc. She apologised to me for how she behaved, what she had said, how she had said it and how she treated me. She remembered that I wouldn't get cross with her, no matter how angry she got, or what she had said. I told her it didn't matter because God so loved her and would always love her. She said, 'That's just what you said last time, I still don't get your God, but you know there must be something?' She gave me a big hug, evidently relieved that she had had an opportunity to apologise.

I would like to say thank you – on Saturday your kindness was much appreciated. We were on our way home after leaving a pub, my feet were so sore and I was walking barefoot. Your kind team stopped to talk to us and gave me a pair of flip flops. I was so grateful, the woman was wonderful. I did tell her it was a night out as I would be going in for surgery after having a cancer scare. She gave me a hug and said a prayer, she made me feel good, and I won't forget it. I wanted to give a donation, but the woman said they could not accept one. Could you please send me an address so that I can donate? Again thank you so much.

They helped my friend's daughter, who was drunk, nineteen and had lost her shoes. Street Pastors came along, gave her a pair of flip flops and made sure she safely got home. It's for that, that I think it's a good idea and for that I'm eternally grateful.

Thanks from the homeless

[A Street Pastor writes] On a recent patrol a young man crossed the road to talk to us, saying, 'You guys do a fantastic job.' He explained that he had been on the streets for five years and said that, 'When you're on the streets and people ignore or maybe kick you for being there, you tend to wonder, what is the point of it all? But you guys come along and give us the time of day and respect us, and it makes you think that maybe there's light at the end of the tunnel after all. You don't know the value of what you do.' He then told the team that he now has a flat and is doing well, and thanked us again.

All the thanks above from members of the public came from Plymouth Street Pastors and are used with kind permission.

Endorsements from the police

Violent offences are 12 to 15 per cent lower than this time last year and I would attribute much of that to what the street pastors [sic] are doing.
Andy Noble, Salisbury Police Inspector – 2012.[180]

In Kingston, after violent crime around the town centre almost halved between 2005 and 2009, *Superintendent Paul McGregor* praised the Street Pastors' 'tremendous work' as a key factor.[181]

[Cheltenham, according to Martin Surl] 'would be much, much harder to police without the street pastors. I used to be a bobby years ago in Cheltenham. It is just such a nicer atmosphere.'
Martin Surl, the Police and Crime Commissioner for Gloucestershire – 2015.[182]

The Reading Street Pastors have been providing an unparalleled service to the community of Reading for ten years.

On what is a momentous anniversary I would both personally and on behalf of Thames Valley Police, like to say what an honour and a privilege it has been to be involved with the Street Pastors, and to have been able to support the organisation and their volunteers.

---

[180] Dan Hitchens, 'Send in the street pastors', *The Spectator*, 5th December, 2015, https://www.spectator.co.uk/article/send-in-the-street-pastors (accessed 8th July 2020).
[181] Ibid. Emphasis ours.
[182] Ibid.

The many exceptional individuals whom have been involved in delivering the ability to protect the vulnerable deserve great thanks for their incredible dedication and hours of voluntary service, often in the early hours of the morning, in bad weather and occasionally dealing with difficult situations that many would shy away from.

The Reading Street Pastors began by providing a service to the Reading night-time economy. This has since expanded to include the railway system, Reading festival, Reading freshers week and Henley Regatta.

The Reading Street Pastors and all involved deserve all the plaudits that this ten year anniversary offers and we sincerely thank you all.

PC Simon Wheeler, working in the night-time economy in Reading, Licensing Officer – October 2019.

I have been responsible for the Neighbourhood Policing Teams within Plymouth City Centre for the last ten years. During that time I have been involved in numerous initiatives and worked with many different voluntary groups.

In my opinion the work of Street Pastors within Plymouth has to be one of the best organised, best supported and most impacting initiatives that I have had the pleasure to work with. You could say that they have been the victim of their own success in that they have had numerous requests from different communities and agencies to patrol their respective neighbourhoods.

Every Saturday night without fail they are on the streets of Plymouth City Centre assisting vulnerable individuals who if left to fend for themselves would be at high risk of becoming a victim of crime. Many of these individuals are very intoxicated or depressed and what they need is someone to talk to, someone to make sure that they don't come to any harm.

In the past these individuals would have been left to fend for themselves or been arrested for their own safety, now there is a third and much better option. As well as being an extra set of eyes and ears on the street their mere presence can often de-fuse [sic] situations.

With the success of the early and night-time economy patrols we have seen Plymouth Street Pastors conduct patrols in other parts of the City where the congregation of large groups of youths were of concern to local residents and more recently we have seen the highly successful introduction of School Pastors to the Plymstock area of Plymouth.

The feedback from this scheme from local businesses and schools has been outstanding. Local police in the area have seen a substantial drop in anti-social behaviour incidents.

Inspector Russell Sharpe (now retired), Neighbourhood Inspector, Plymouth City Centre – circa 2010.[183]

Do we [Street Pastors] provide value for money? While our aim is simply to care for people in whatever way we can, we have been grateful to learn that what we do can save time and money for the police, the NHS and the

---

[183] 'A Police Perspective: Plymouth Street Pastors', https://streetpastors.org/locations/plymouth/street-stories/a-police-perspective-plymouth-street-pastors/ (accessed 8th July 2020).

courts. We were once asked by one of our funding assistants if we could quantify how much we might save the police, as it may help with some of our grant applications, so we asked a local Police Inspector for his opinion.

Inspector Russell Sharpe comments, 'It would be difficult to quantify how much you save us. If you were to look at a simple offence like being drunk, it would probably take an officer a minimum of two hours to complete the booking in procedure and the paperwork. The individual would then remain in custody overnight, which would also [incur] additional expense as he would have [to] be closely observed because of his intoxicated state. So a simple drunk would probably cost us several hundred pounds. If he was charged to court this would increase into the thousands.

'If you were able to prevent a serious assault you would save us thousands of pounds, the health service tens of thousands and the Criminal Justice System tens of thousands of pounds. If you managed to prevent a sexual assault you would also save us thousands of pounds.'

Inspector Russell Sharpe (now retired), Neighbourhood Inspector, Plymouth City Centre – circa 2010.[184]

A few stories from the press

The stories below are from 2004 to 2019. Brief details of each story only are given. The full stories or articles can be found online.

---

[184] Plymouth Street Pastors, 'Value for Money',
https://streetpastors.org/locations/plymouth/donate/value-for-money/
(accessed 8th July 2020).

2004 – 'Street pastors on a mission from God' – BBC News online.[185]

This article discusses the origins of Street Pastors, in particular that the initiative began in Kingston, Jamaica.

2008 – 'Street pastors making a difference after-hours' – *The Telegraph*.[186]

In June 2008, *The Telegraph* newspaper wrote an article with the title 'Street pastors making a difference after-hours'. The article quoted David Cameron as saying, 'It's absolutely fantastic the job the Street Pastors are doing. What we need is more people out in the community supporting the police, who can't do the job of beating antisocial behaviour on their own.'

Boris Johnson, then the Mayor of London, was also quoted as referring to the 'extraordinary and inspiring movement' of Street Pastors, which he saw as a key part of reducing violence on the streets.

---

[185] Dominic Casciani, 'Street pastors on a mission from God', BBC News, 5th November 2004, http://news.bbc.co.uk/1/hi/uk/2834993.stm (accessed 8th July 2020).

[186] Rowena Mason, 'Street pastors making a difference after-hours', *The Telegraph*, 1st June 2008, https://www.telegraph.co.uk/news/uknews/2059652/Street-pastors-help-young-revellers-on-their-way.html (accessed 8th July 2020).

2014 – 'Know thy selfie: Archbishop of Canterbury poses for pictures with clubbers during late-night stint as street pastor in Bristol' – *Mail Online*.[187]

The article describes when Justin Welby, Archbishop of Canterbury, headed out onto the streets of Bristol to meet Saturday night revellers, as a Street Pastors observer.

2015 – 'Send in the street pastors' – *The Spectator*[188]

The Spectator magazine of December 2015 devotes an article to summarising the work of Street Pastors. The piece includes praise for the work of Street Pastors from the three different police officers Andy Noble, Paul McGregor and Martin Surl, as mentioned earlier.

The author comments on the overall effect of Street Pastors: 'The results of these accumulated tiny gestures are remarkable. Since 2003, when the initiative was founded (they are now active in over 280 UK locations), Street Pastors have been repeatedly credited with reducing crime.'

---

[187] Mark Duell, 'Know thy selfie: Archbishop of Canterbury poses for pictures with clubbers during late-night stint as street pastor in Bristol', *Mail Online*, 15th September 2014, https://www.dailymail.co.uk/news/article-2756636/Know-thy-selfie-Archbishop-Canterbury-poses-pictures-clubbers-late-night-stint-street-pastor-Bristol.html (accessed 8th July 2020).

[188] Dan Hitchens, 'Send in the street pastors', *The Spectator*, 5th December 2015, https://www.spectator.co.uk/article/send-in-the-street-pastors (accessed 8th July 2020).

2016 – 'Street pastors will save NHS £13million during festive period' – *Premier Christian News*[189]

Rev Les Isaac, during an interview with Antony Bushfield (*Premier Christian News*), commented that a council leader in one area had told him that Street Pastors had saved the NHS about £6,000 in one night. This was because in this area, Street Pastors was running a 'safe space' where people who were intoxicated were helped, without needing to go to A&E. Les went on to say that Street Pastors was saving the NHS millions of pounds every year.

As part of the article, Antony went on to do a calculation, stating, 'According to NHS Digital, the NHS treated 67,730 people in December 2015 who had been admitted to hospital partly because of alcohol, at an average cost of £4,296 each.' He went on to estimate that if each of the 300 Street Pastors groups across the country, during each of the ten Fridays and Saturdays during the festive period of December, stopped just one person ending up in A&E, it would save 10 x 300 x £4,296, or almost £13 million.

---

[189] Antony Bushfield, 'Street pastors will save NHS £13million during festive period', *Premier Christian News*, 15th December 2016, https://premierchristian.news/en/news/article/street-pastors-will-save-nhs-13million-during-festive-period (accessed 8th July 2020).

2018 – '"I'll ask God to intervene": the Christian volunteers doing police work in Reading – video', *The Guardian*[190]

A ten-minute video produced by *The Guardian* newspaper, filmed in Reading town centre on the 28th and 29th of September 2018. Worth watching.

The film illustrates the way in which Street Pastors assists Thames Valley Police in the town centre on Friday and Saturday nights. This includes keeping an eye out for trouble and known criminals, as well as helping very drunk people who would otherwise take up police time. It even provides a taxi service for individuals who are so drunk that most taxi drivers would not accept them.

2019 – 'Saddleworth street pastors aiming for first patrol' – *The Oldham Times*[191]

The local newspaper recorded that the first Street Pastors team in Greater Manchester started in 2004 in Moss Side and that teams now operated across the area, including Failsworth, Chadderton, Stalybridge, Bury and Rochdale.

Saddleworth is about nine miles from the city centre of Manchester. The article went on to say that the first official patrol in Saddleworth would be 14th June 2019.

---

[190] '"I'll ask God to intervene": the Christian volunteers doing police work in Reading – video', *The Guardian*, 18th December 2018, https://www.theguardian.com/uk-news/video/2018/dec/18/ill-ask-god-to-intervene-the-christian-volunteers-doing-police-work-in-reading-video (accessed 8th July 2020).

[191] Nick Jackson, 'Saddleworth street pastors aiming for first patrol', *The Oldham Times*, 7th May 2019, https://www.theoldhamtimes.co.uk/news/17623236.saddleworth-street-pastors-aiming-for-first-patrol/?ref=rss (accessed 8th July 2020).

2019 – 'Weymouth Street Pastors have handed out nearly 5,000 flip flops to town's revellers' – *Dorset Echo*[192]

Weymouth Street Pastors was launched in 2008, and by October 2019 it had given out 4,743 pairs of flip flops.

2019 – 'Street Pastor saves life after spotting man floating in Torquay harbour' – *Devon Live*[193]

The article commented that a member of a Street Pastors team had found a coat and a pair of trainers on a bench in the early hours of one Sunday morning.

In looking for the owner, one of the team spotted a body face up in the Torquay harbour. The team called 999, resulting in the man being rescued alive and taken to hospital.

Awards

Other ways to gauge the positive effects of Street Pastors in the UK include some of the awards received. The awards below are only a small sample taken from some of the areas represented in this book.

In 2018, Reading Street Pastors received two awards. One was the Area Commanders Commendation from Thames

[192] Sam Beamish, 'Weymouth Street Pastors have handed out nearly 5,000 flip flops to town's revellers', *Dorset Echo*, 21st October 2019, https://www.dorsetecho.co.uk/news/17981339.weymouth-street-pastors-handed-nearly-5-000-flip-flops-towns-revellers/ (accessed 8th July 2020).
[193] Colleen Smith, 'Street Pastor saves life after spotting man floating in Torquay harbour', *Devon Live*, 23rd October 2019, https://www.devonlive.com/news/devon-news/street-pastor-saves-life-after-3459251 (accessed 8th July 2020).

Valley Police. The second award was Volunteer of the Year award, from Pride of Reading.

In 2019, Plymouth was presented with Purple Flag status, an award given to cities and towns that surpass the standards of excellence in managing their evening and night-time economy. The various organisations that presented to the assessors stressed that the unity between their groups, which include **Street Pastors**, was the main reason why the night-time economy worked so well

In 2016, Street Pastors Kingston received an award for Outstanding Contribution to the Night-time Economy.

A small research study

In 2011/12, a study at Kingston University was carried out by Sylvia Collins-May, Andrew King and Lee Jones on the social and spiritual impact of Street Pastors in one London Borough.[194]

In this particular area, most Street Pastors are middle-aged or older.

The key findings of the study were:

- 'Street Pastors improves individuals' safety and wellbeing in the immediate context of a night patrol by "domesticating the streets."'

---

[194] Sylvia Collins-May, Andrew King and Lee Jones, 'Faith in Action: Street Pastors Kingston Social and Spiritual Impact Project', Kingston University 2012. Unpublished. Used with permission.

- 'Being middle or older aged can be an advantage to volunteers when engaging with members of the public.'

- 'Street Pastors helps to reduce opportunities for antisocial behaviour. Low level interventions and interruptions reduce the potential for problems on the streets.'

- 'Street Pastors volunteers are increasingly recognised, respected, valued and trusted by members of the public and personnel in partner organisations.'

- 'Street Pastors volunteers utilise "spiritual resources" in their pastoral work to attend to people's existential questions and need for spiritual comfort, while maintaining a boundary between normative Christian mission and proselytising.'

The study did not include the significant input that Street Pastors can have in supporting the homeless in many areas, as has been mentioned in parts of this book, in particular Chapter 5.

Chapter 19
The Story of the Loving Father

Street Pastors are often asked or told, 'Why do you do this? You look old enough to be my gran! You should be tucked up in bed in the early hours of the morning,' or similar. It is usually inappropriate to give a long-winded answer, although sometimes a brief reply leads to further conversation and genuine interest.

This book started with the story of the Good Samaritan, and now concludes with another story that Jesus told, about a good and loving father, in an attempt to answer why Street Pastors do what they do, from a different perspective.

The French author and novelist Abbé Prévost, who lived in the eighteenth century, is recorded as saying, 'The heart of a father is the masterpiece of nature.'[195] No doubt something of this father's heart prompted Pat Barrett to write the Christian song 'Good, Good Father', which was then sung by Chris Tomlin and first released in 2015. Pat Barrett was originally inspired to write it by his own role as a father, and said, 'When I started having

---

[195] Antoine François Prévost, Goodreads, https://www.goodreads.com/author/show/8563709.Antoine_Fran_ois_Pr_vost (accessed 8th July 2020).

kids and I'm looking at my daughter Harper Gray, and I'm like, how am I going to explain God to you?'[196]

Of course, others have different views of God and fathers. *New York Times* best-selling author Jodi Picoult, in her novel *Keeping Faith*, writes:

> 'I always wondered why God was supposed to be a father,' she whispers. 'Fathers always want you to measure up to something. Mothers are the ones who love you unconditionally, don't you think?'[197]

There are also parts of the Bible that support the view that God has loving attributes of both father and mother, such as, 'As a mother comforts her child, so I'll comfort you.'[198]

Others hold stronger views. The Christian author Alister McGrath in his book *The Dawkins Delusion?: Atheist Fundamentalism and the Denial of the Divine* refers to Richard Dawkins' view of God as unforgiving, vindictive, bloodthirsty and many other negatives.[199] Alister McGrath makes the point that as Richard Dawkins does not believe in God, his opinion is perhaps academic on the subject. McGrath goes on to say that neither he nor anyone he knows believes in the God Dawkins describes.[200]

---

[196] Song Facts, https://www.songfacts.com/facts/chris-tomlin/good-good-father (accessed 1st October 2020).
[197] p 91 from *Keeping Faith* by Jodi Picoult. Copyright (c) 1999 by Jodi Picoult. Used with the permission of HarperCollins Publishers.
[198] Isaiah 66:13.
[199] Alister E McGrath and Joanna C McGrath, *The Dawkins Delusion?: Atheist Fundamentalism and the Denial of the Divine* (London: IVP Books, 2010).
[200] Ibid.

Contrary to Dawkins' view of the God he does not believe in, the first chapter of this book focuses on one of the stories Jesus told, known as the story of the Good Samaritan, and how this simple story has possibly been an influence in many 'Good Samaritan' initiatives across the world. This story points to the character of God, in that Jesus used the story to teach how we should love and care for our neighbours.

One of the other best-known stories that Jesus told, which also points to the character of God as loving, is the story of the Prodigal Son.[201]

This story has inspired art, popular songs and literature, such as paintings by Rembrandt,[202] one of the most performed Irish folk songs, *The Wild Rover*,[203] and the book *The Return of the Prodigal Son: A Story of Homecoming*[204] by Henri Nouwen, who was a professor and a writer as well as a Dutch Catholic priest, and was inspired to write the book having seen the Rembrandt painting.

The story as it occurs in *The Message* version of the Bible is given below.[205]

---

[201] Luke 15:11-32.

[202] Roland E Fleischer and Susan C Scott, *Rembrandt, Rubens, and the Art of their Time: Recent Perspectives* (Pennsylvania, PA: Pennsylvania State University Press, 1997).

[203] "Wild Rover, the Most Widely Performed Irish Song?', Irish Music Daily, https://www.irishmusicdaily.com/wild-rover (accessed 8th July 2020).

[204] Henri Nouwen, *The Return of the Prodigal Son: A Story of Homecoming* (London: Darton, Longman & Todd, 1994).

[205] Luke 15:11-32.

Then [Jesus] said, 'There was once a man who had two sons. The younger said to his father, "Father, I want right now what's coming to me."

'So the father divided the property between them. It wasn't long before the younger son packed his bags and left for a distant country. There, undisciplined and dissipated, he wasted everything he had. After he had gone through all his money, there was a bad famine all through that country and he began to hurt. He signed on with a citizen there who assigned him to his fields to slop the pigs. He was so hungry he would have eaten the corn-cobs in the pig slop, but no one would give him any.

'That brought him to his senses. He said, "All those farmhands working for my father sit down to three meals a day, and here I am starving to death. I'm going back to my father. I'll say to him, Father, I've sinned against God, I've sinned before you; I don't deserve to be called your son. Take me on as a hired hand." He got right up and went home to his father.

'When he was still a long way off, his father saw him. His heart pounding, he ran out, embraced him, and kissed him. The son started his speech: "Father, I've sinned against God, I've sinned before you; I don't deserve to be called your son ever again."

'But the father wasn't listening. He was calling to the servants, "Quick. Bring a clean set of clothes and dress him. Put the family ring on his finger and sandals on his feet. Then get a grain-fed heifer and roast it. We're going to feast! We're going to have a wonderful time! My son is here – given up for dead and now alive! Given up for lost and now found!" And they began to have a wonderful time.

'All this time his older son was out in the field. When the day's work was done he came in. As he approached the house, he heard the music and dancing. Calling over one of the houseboys, he asked what was going on. He told him, "Your brother came home. Your father has ordered a feast – barbecued beef! – because he has him home safe and sound."

'The older brother stalked off in an angry sulk and refused to join in. His father came out and tried to talk to him, but he wouldn't listen. The son said, "Look how many years I've stayed here serving you, never giving you one moment of grief, but have you ever thrown a party for me and my friends? Then this son of your who has thrown away your money on whores shows up and you go all out with a feast!"

'His father said, "Son, you don't understand. You're with me all the time, and everything that is mine is yours – but this is a wonderful time, and we had to celebrate. This brother of yours was dead, and he's alive! He was lost, and he's found!"'

Like the Good Samaritan, there are many different interpretations of this parable, and it needs to be remembered that the story was told within a Jewish culture about 2,000 years ago.

Taking the story at face value, the father was looking out for the return of his son and was overjoyed to see him. There were no recriminations that the son had squandered his inheritance, but instead a banquet was prepared for him.

In some sermons, the elder, rather disgruntled, son is said to represent someone who feels they have the higher moral ground; possibly a churchgoer, who has attended church for years and served God out of duty, but has for some time forgotten that God loves them for who they are, not for what they do.

New York Times best-seller Timothy Keller in his short book *The Prodigal God*[206] explains the meaning behind the story in more detail. In particular, he comments that the elder son is said to represent the religious people or Pharisees of the day. So one son has gone off the rails with a wayward lifestyle, and the other son, because he is so upright and proud, has a cold heart to both his brother and his father.

Timothy Keller points out that the story is in a chapter with two other stories about something lost, one being a lost sheep, the other a lost coin. In both of these stories the lost item is searched for, and when found there is a celebration.[207] He then contrasts these two stories to the story of the Prodigal Son, and suggests that a true elder brother would have gone and looked for his younger brother.

[206] Timothy Keller, *The Prodigal God* (London: Hodder & Stoughton, 2008).
[207] Luke 15:1-10.

How do both of these passages of the Bible fit with what Street Pastors does?

For some Street Pastors, whether consciously or unconsciously, there may be a sense of duty to be a 'Good Samaritan' that is an inspiration or motive to be out on the streets till the early hours.

Doing things only out of a sense of duty can become tedious, though, and the story of the Prodigal Son (or the loving father) suggests a motive beyond duty alone. God loves and cares for all those people out on the streets, whether they are drunk or sober, rich or poor, and whatever religion, social class, sexual orientation, ethnic background and more.

In addition to a sense of duty to help out and make a difference if possible, for most Street Pastors, caring for others is probably related to some understanding of God's love for them as individuals and a belief in the reality of the love of God for all humanity. They realise that they are not superior to those they are trying to help, but are just as much in need of God's love. This motivation may be especially strong for parents who have worried about teenage or older children at times, aware of some of the possible pitfalls of being young and out very late.

Stories can be powerful ways to put across concepts. Returning to the Prodigal Son (or the loving father), it is a simple but powerful illustration of the unconditional love of a father for both of his sons. This can, of course, be applied to fathers and daughters, mothers and sons, mothers and daughters and more. Perhaps there is something of Street Pastors representing more of a true elder brother that Timothy Keller describes in the Prodigal Son passage when they embark on helping those in need.

Jesus was telling the story to illustrate how God loves us. Now, about 2,000 years later, it has not lost its power. We do not need a degree or a doctorate in theology to get the message.

This short book gives a snapshot of stories from the work of Street Pastors, School Pastors, Response Pastors and Rail Pastors. There could be hundreds more, and each week there will be new ones. Some will be similar to those told here, but some will be new and different. Some may appear trivial; others could be life-changing or life-saving.

The nineteenth-century English poet Elizabeth Barrett Browning wrote in one of her poems:

Earth's crammed with heaven,
And every common bush afire with God,
But only he who sees takes off his shoes;
The rest sit round and pluck blackberries.[208]

This poem refers to a part in the Bible where Moses sees God in a burning bush that does not burn away and is told, 'Don't come any closer. Remove your sandals from your feet. You're standing on holy ground.'[209]

Perhaps metaphorically in some sort of way, we need to look closely to 'see' the Father heart of God behind the

[208] Elizabeth Barrett Browning, 'Aurora Leigh', in *The Oxford Book of English Mystical Verse* (Oxford: Clarendon Press, 1945).
[209] Exodus 3:5.

giving out of flips flops at 3am, offering a sick bag or a wet wipe to someone, sitting down and talking to a homeless person, or listening to someone who may be suicidal on a railway station.

While it may seem irreverent to make such an analogy, perhaps such encounters are in some way holy encounters. Jesus Himself did not hold back from helping people on the streets from all sorts of backgrounds with a wide array of life and health issues, and He taught that we should follow His example.

Street Pastors shows in practical ways that Christians do care for others and are prepared to get out of their comfort zones to show this. The motivation comes from a God whose character is love,[210] and who is concerned for individuals, as told in the stories of the Good Samaritan and of the loving father.

We hope you have enjoyed reading this book and have found interesting some of the contemporary stories it contains.

---

[210] See 1 John 4:8.

Conclusion

In less than twenty years, Street Pastors has become a respected organisation, caring for others in hundreds of towns and cities across the UK, and in other countries also.

As an organisation, it is widely endorsed and supported by the public, the police and politicians, with a few examples of endorsements given in this book.

But what has contributed to the success of Street Pastors?

Perhaps, firstly, the Street Pastors' story is a very human one. It is about individuals giving up time to receive training, and with this training going to the streets, railway stations and schools to care, listen and help others.

Initial and ongoing training, supervision, accountability, mentoring, prayer and pastoral support are no doubt key factors to the success of Street Pastors, making sure volunteers are both suitably trained and supported. This training makes it possible for Christians to show practical care for others outside their normal church, home, work, college, etc, and perhaps outside their comfort zones.

Perhaps, secondly, one of the main reasons for the success of Street Pastors is that its ethos is to offer non-judgemental and unconditional support, care and help to people, regardless of race, religion, wealth, sexual orientation, etc.

While Street Pastors is a Christian organisation, and the Christian ethos of both the organisation and the individual volunteers is part of the very DNA that makes Street Pastors what it is, the care it offers is not linked to a requirement to share the Christian message, over and above the practical message of care and love to individuals. This probably helps people feel safe, that they are going to be helped and supported, not preached at and judged. This does not negate the pastoral care Street Pastors show to people, and many people on the streets accept prayer, and thus a certain level of spiritual input.

Rev Les Isaac in an interview said, 'Over the years I've had some really negative letters from Christians who think that we should only be preaching the gospel. But there are so many stories of people saying, "Because of you guys, I've gone back to church," or, "I've found Jesus because of you."'[211]

And, of course, as the stories of the Good Samaritan and the Prodigal Son both illustrate, God wants to reach out and help people, and there are no strings attached to

---

[211] Bernard Hibbs, 'Equipped with Water, Flip-Flops and Prayer', *Plough Quarterly Magazine*, No. 6, Autumn 2015,
https://www.plough.com/en/topics/life/work/equipped-with-water-flip-flops-and-prayer (accessed 8th July 2020).

His love. This book illustrates many such stories of love in action.

If you would like to volunteer as a Prayer or Street Pastor, or if you would like to go out as an observer one night, do visit the website at https://www.streetpastors.org for further details.

For details of initiatives in your areas, see https://www.streetpastors.org/our-network/united-kingdom/ and then follow links to initiatives in different locations.

Finally, to conclude, Mother Teresa once said, 'At first I thought I had to convert. Then I learned that my task is to love.'[212]

---

[212] W Bader (ed), William Hartnett (trans), *Like a Drop in the Ocean: 99 Saying by Mother Teresa* (New York, NY: New City Press, 2006), p 63.

Brief update post-Covid-19
July 2020

Owing to the spread of Covid-19 in the UK, on Monday 23rd March 2020, the prime minister, Boris Johnson, placed the UK on lockdown. This meant that all but essential businesses were to close with immediate effect. Members of the public were to stay in their homes except for essential work, to shop for essentials or to go out in certain circumstances, including one form of daily exercise.

In Edinburgh, Glasgow, Plymouth, Reading and Taunton, five areas mentioned earlier in this book, all patrols stopped during lockdown. This was in line with government policy, but also because the night-time economy had stopped.

As restrictions began to lift in June, Plymouth, Reading and Taunton all became involved in daytime patrols following government social distancing guidelines.

In Plymouth, this involved patrols along the seafront on Friday and Saturday afternoons.

In Reading, Street Pastors teams have been going out from Monday to Friday between 10am and 2pm at the request of the town centre police. The aim has been to look out for lonely, vulnerable people and people who may have mental health issues, with a view to signposting them to relevant agencies. In particular, Reading Street Pastors spent many hours in Forbury Gardens Public Park after three fatal stabbings occurred on June 20th,[213] and also had a presence at a private vigil in response.

In Taunton, again after some easing of lockdown and with the encouragement and blessing of the neighbourhood police sergeant, a new daytime patrol in the town centre park has been initiated and Street Pastors are back patrolling on two housing estates during the day and early evenings.

With pubs reopening on the 4th July, Street Pastors groups are assessing how they can be safely deployed again in the night-time economy.

Let's conclude with a heart-warming post-lockdown story:

> A long-standing homeless person in our town stopped and greeted me warmly. The Street Pastors have engaged with him on and off for about twelve years. A heroin addict and alcohol-dependent, with a track record of problems, he has been housed in an amazing temporary hostel. The hostel offered a great programme of support and creative activities and this man was doing art there.

---

[213] Natasha Turak, 'Deadly stabbing attack in UK's Reading is a terrorist incident, police say', CNBC, 21st June 2020, https://www.cnbc.com/2020/06/21/police-treat-uk-deadly-stabbing-spree-as-terrorism-incident.html (accessed 4th July 2020).

It was lovely to see him sober and so positive, especially at midday, by which time he would previously be semiconscious, lying in a side alley somewhere. He departed cheerfully, saying he loved me!